Wedding Etiquette

Other Titles in *The Wedding Collection*:

The Complete Wedding Organiser and Record
The Best Man's Organiser
Wedding Speeches and Toasts
The Best Best Man
Mitch Murray's One-Liners for Weddings
Your Wedding Planner

Wedding Etiquette

PAT AND BILL DERRAUGH

foulsham
LONDON • NEW YORK • TORONTO • SYDNEY

foulsham

The Publishing House, Bennetts Close,
Cippenham, Berkshire, SL1 5AP, England

While every effort has been made to ensure the accuracy of all the information contained within this book, neither the authors nor the publisher can be liable for any errors. In particular, since laws change from time to time, it is vital that each individual should check relevant legal details for himself or herself.

ISBN 0-572-02409-6

Printed in Great Britain by
Cox & Wyman Ltd, Reading, Berkshire

CONTENTS

INTRODUCTION

There are many ways of getting married and of celebrating the occasion: from the traditional 'white wedding' followed by a grand reception attended by all known friends and relatives, to the register office ceremony with just a selected few present.

Times and fashions change and 'courtship' as it was once known has taken on a different form, but despite a modern approach to many traditional customs the wedding still retains a great deal of its former sense of occasion. Many brides cherish dreams of an idyllic wedding day; dreams which could sway them towards a church wedding rather than one conducted by a registrar.

Although couples today are unlikely to follow custom slavishly, many find that wedding tradition and the ceremony of wedding etiquette enhances the occasion. Whilst the rules concerning the responsibilities and duties of wedding party members have been relaxed and the days when wedding preparations were entirely the job of the bride and her mother are long gone, couples still find that etiquette and their family's views are important considerations.

This book is for those who want to know about the protocol, formalities, the long-established customs and traditional order of events expected at a wedding. However, it is obviously the couple's decision as to how much they want to conform, bearing in mind that weddings are more flexible than they were in the past and it is not necessary to be ruled by convention; if the bride does not want a veil she need not have one; similarly if a buffet seems preferable to a formal meal then this should be the choice.

The overall organisation of the occasion falls to the bride and groom but other people involved, such as the best man, the bride's mother and father and the bridesmaids will need to be aware of their duties and may find this book useful.

With the changing nature of our modern world it will sometimes be the woman who proposes marriage, but whoever does the asking, if the answer is yes, then it is just the beginning of what could be a wonderful life together. To start the adventure off smoothly you will find this book invaluable in helping you to organise the wedding day.

There are so many details to remember in the planning process that it is a good idea to have an *aide-mémoire* to ensure that nothing is overlooked. We have therefore included checklists at the end of the relevant chapters which can be used to tick off each completed job. There are different lists for the principal participants and events, and any items on the lists which are not relevant can easily be deleted.

Here's hoping that your wedding day goes as planned and that this book helps to make your big day memorable!

1

GETTING ENGAGED

In 'the good old days' when grandma was a girl, there were strict conventions on the subject of marriage. It is more than likely that any young man she was 'walking out with' may even have been selected by her father through an arrangement with one of his friends or colleagues who had a son who could be considered acceptable in terms of family, prospects and finances.

If the young man was suitably smitten, after a decent interval he would approach her father and ask that he be allowed to ask for his daughter's hand in marriage. If permission was given, he would make his formal proposal, probably going down on one knee, and hopefully she would say yes.

Times have changed and young people nowadays have many more opportunities to meet, socially and at work. They enjoy far more freedom, and when it comes to choosing a marriage partner and 'popping the question' it is their own choice. The man might still propose on bended knee, but the general approach to marriage is far less formal than it used to be. The couple may often have been living together for a while.

Although these days it is the exception rather than the rule, taking the trouble to ask the woman's father is still one of the best ways of establishing an amicable son-in-law/father-in-law relationship. It is just as important today to ensure that there are no absolute objections to the marriage and that the bride's parents are satisfied that their prospective son-in-law can provide happiness and support for their daughter.

Whatever the circumstances leading up to the engagement, they should not detract from the fact that the couple have decided that they want to make a permanent commitment to each other and naturally now want everybody to know that they intend to get married.

Breaking the News

The first people to be told the news should be the bride's parents and then the groom's parents. For most weddings it is unlikely that the bride's father will be asked for his consent, although the law requires that in England and Wales the consent of parents or guardians is obtained for marriage if either party is under the age of 18. They must be over 16. In Scotland the requirement is that they may marry provided they are both at least 16 years old on the day of their marriage.

After both sets of parents have been told, a general announcement can be made, usually by word of mouth to relatives and close friends. This will need to be done fairly quickly, to beat the grapevine! Most couples like to inform close relatives and friends personally or by telephone, and many write to other relations and friends announcing their engagement and giving a few details about their fiancé(e) and future plans. If writing, all letters should be posted at the same time so that no one feels excluded. A tick-list will help to keep track of those informed.

It is only natural that when a couple become engaged they want the whole world to know, but the announcement should not be made at someone else's wedding.

The formality of an announcement in the press is much rarer than it used to be. However, some couples like to announce their engagement in the national press, but for most an entry in the local paper is sufficient. (It is proper to inform relatives and close friends in advance.) The bride's mother or the prospective bride sends the announcement to the editor.

Here is an example for a formal announcement:

Mr R. Brown and Miss/Ms P. Smith
The engagement is announced between
Robert
only son of
Mr and Mrs Richard Brown of Queensgrove
and
Patricia
youngest daughter of
Mr and Mrs David Smith of Kingsgrove

It would be bad form to announce the intention to marry again while still married to a former partner.

The Engagement Ring

Traditionally the man gives his future bride a ring to wear as a sign of their engagement. A gold ring, with one or more diamonds, is probably the most popular design, but it is entirely a matter of choice. The days when a man produced a ring and placed it on his future bride's finger directly she had accepted his proposal are virtually over. This may happen if he has a family ring which he wants her to have, but more often than not they will find it best to choose the engagement ring together.

The cost of rings varies enormously and it will depend on personal circumstances and future plans as to how much should be spent. If the engagement is to be a short one the decision may be to limit spending on a ring and be in a better financial position to meet the numerous costs that the couple will have.

The selection of styles and settings of rings is huge, so it is as well to have some idea of what is available in your price range before setting foot in the shop, otherwise there is a risk of being tempted to exceed your budget.

Apart from the traditional diamond engagement ring there are many attractive alternatives, and birthstones are a popular choice.

The various stones are said to symbolise particular qualities:

January	Garnet for constancy
February	Amethyst for sincerity
March	Bloodstone for courage
April	Diamond for innocence
May	Emerald for success
June	Pearl for health
July	Ruby for love
August	Sardonyx for married happiness
September	Sapphire for wisdom
October	Opal for hope
November	Topaz for fidelity
December	Turquoise for harmony

Many women like to give a present in return to mark this very special occasion. Suggestions for such a gift include a gold signet ring, gold chain, tie-clip or cuff-links.

The Engagement Party

Some couples announce their engagement officially – and as a surprise – at a party traditionally given by the bride's parents who, along with the groom's parents, already know the news. Today, guests are usually tipped off in advance, however. The bride's father makes the official announcement at the celebration and the bride's mother issues the invitations. These need not be printed; they can be handwritten letters or cards, or a telephone call would suffice.

If there is to be a formal engagement party, the engagement ring is not worn in public until the announcement is made.

The engagement party should be held fairly shortly after the announcement is made so that it will serve as a suitable opportunity for congratulations and good wishes to be heaped on the happy couple – together with a few presents, no doubt!

The engagement party guest list may often be composed almost entirely of relations and can serve as an ideal opportunity for the prospective bride and groom to meet their future in-laws.

The home of the bride's parents is often the venue for the

engagement party and traditionally the bride's father will bear the cost, although nowadays it is more likely that the cost will be shared, perhaps by the groom's father, who might also offer to hold the party at his home. Alternatively, it may be decided to hold the party in a hall if there is a more extensive guest list, or to celebrate the occasion with a small dinner party in a restaurant with just immediate family and friends. Wherever it is held it should be an informal affair with just two speeches: the bride's father announcing the engagement and the bridegroom-to-be on behalf of his bride and himself proposing the health of their parents.

The party is an ideal opportunity for the two sets of parents to meet if they have not done so already, but if they live too great a distance apart for one set of parents to attend the party, the newly engaged pair should visit them as soon as possible so that they will see the couple and celebrate with them in a small way.

'Showers'

'Showers' are parties for women. They are given by someone in honour of the prospective bride and usually held during the daytime at a friend's home. At the shower, small gifts are offered to the bride. These can have themes, for example, 'kitchen shower', 'bedroom shower'.

Breaking Off the Engagement

If, for some reason, the bride and groom decide not to proceed with the wedding, engagement gifts received from relatives or friends should be returned. If the two parties are still friends, they may decide to keep any presents given to each other during their time together, although etiquette demands that the girl offers to return the ring, especially if she is the one to break off the engagement. It is the man's decision whether to accept it or not; if it is a family heirloom or his mother's engagement ring, he will most probably want to do so.

Relatives and friends can be informed quietly. The traditional approach is to make an announcement in the press which simply states the names and that the wedding will not take place.

An engagement to marry is no longer a binding contract in the eyes of the law and nowadays we have a more philosophical approach to a break-up at this stage; far better to find out now, we say, than to have regrets after the wedding.

CHECKLIST: THE ENGAGEMENT

- Announce decision to her parents ☐
- Announce decision to his parents ☐
- Arrange for parents to meet ☐
- Buy the ring ☐
  - Traditional ring ☐
  - Family ring or heirloom ☐
  - Antique ring ☐
  - Birthstone ☐
- Present from her to him ☐
  Although not necessary, a ring, cuff-links or similar gift, preferably of gold or silver, is acceptable
- Tell relatives ☐
- Tell close friends ☐
- Engagement party/celebration ☐
- Press announcement ☐

2

WHAT THE LAW SAYS ABOUT MARRIAGE

There are many ways, civil and religious, of taking the all-important step of getting married. This chapter deals with them mainly from the legal aspect.

ENGLAND AND WALES

In England and Wales a marriage can take place by means of (a) a ceremony performed in accordance with the rites of the Church of England, (b) a civil ceremony, or (c) a ceremony performed in accordance with the rites of a religious denomination other than the Church of England.

CHURCH OF ENGLAND

A marriage in accordance with the rites of the Church of England may be contracted in one of four ways:

1. By publication of banns.
2. By common licence (ordinary licence).
3. By special licence.
4. On the authority of a certificate issued by a Superintendent Registrar.

Generally, only one party to the marriage will be required to be a member of the Church of England and at least one of them should live in the parish of the church where the marriage is to take place (although certain residence exceptions may be made, for example, in the case of marriage by special licence or sometimes if a person is an established member of a church outside his or her home parish and has his or her name entered on the electoral roll of that parish).

Although divorced people may remarry under civil law in the presence of a registrar, the Church does not allow the remarriage of divorced people in church. Nevertheless, some ministers will agree to conduct a church wedding given these circumstances, but the normal procedure, if the couple really want the blessing of the Church, is to have a civil wedding with just a few close friends and relatives in attendance, followed by a Service of Blessing in church, possibly attended by many more family and friends. In this way the ceremony and sense of occasion are maintained.

1. ***Publication of Banns:*** This is the method traditionally preferred by most people. The first thing to do is to call upon the minister of the church in which the marriage is to be solemnised and to ask him or her to allow the ceremony to take place in their church. If you would like another minister to officiate at the wedding (an old friend of the family, for example) that should also be discussed. When all the preliminaries have been satisfactorily completed, the minister will proceed to publish the banns.

The banns are published by being read aloud in church on three successive Sundays preceding the ceremony. They are usually read at the main church service. It is usual for the couple to be in church on at least one of the three occasions when the banns are read.

When the couple do not live in the same parish, the banns must be read in duplicate (a) in the man's parish and (b) in the woman's parish. A certificate should be obtained from the minister whose church is not being used to give to the minister in whose church the ceremony is to take place. This certificate states that the banns have been legally called; without it the officiating minister cannot proceed with the wedding service.

Once the banns have been published, the wedding may be solemnised on any day within the three following months. It is best not to leave it too late. Marriages sometimes have to be delayed, and if there is insufficient time to arrange an alternative date within the three months the banns will have to be called again.

Since the system of marriage by banns has been devised to give publicity to the forthcoming wedding, it is fraudulent to substitute misleading names for the proper ones. When a person is generally known by a name which is not the one shown on his or her birth certificate, the banns should give the name more generally known, or should include both.

2. ***Common Licence (Ordinary Licence):*** The advantages of being married by common licence are that banns are unnecessary and only one clear day's notice is needed before the licence to marry is issued. It is therefore a much quicker procedure, and especially useful when for some reason the banns have not been properly published.

Common licences may be obtained from one of the Surrogates who grant licences in the diocese. The minister at the church where the wedding is to take place may hold this title; if he or she does not, they will be able to tell you where you can obtain the licence.

In applying at any of the above offices, it is necessary that one of the parties to the marriage should appear in person. The person making the application is required to sign a declaration stating that there is no legal reason why the marriage cannot properly take place and that either the man or the woman, or both, have lived for at least 15 days prior to the application within the area served by the church that is to be used for the ceremony.

3. ***Special Licence:*** Special licences are issued only on the authority of the Archbishop of Canterbury from The Registrar of the Court of Faculties, 1 The Sanctuary, Westminster, London SW1P 3JT, telephone 0171 222 5381, and in cases when there is some special and urgent reason why the more ordinary methods of solemnising the marriage are unsuitable. When granted, a special licence permits the wedding to take place at any time (within three months of the date of issue) and in any place, without restriction as to the residence of either party.

4. ***Superintendent Registrar's Certificate:*** A certificate to marry in accordance with the rites of the Church of England may also be given by a Superintendent Registrar.

The church where the marriage is to take place must be situated within the registration district of the Superintendent Registrar and either the man or the woman must have lived in the parish for seven days prior to giving notice.

The certificate will not be issued until 21 days after the notice is entered in the notice book and the ceremony may then take place within three months from the day on which the notice was entered. The marriage may be solemnised only by a minister of the Church of England and with the consent of the minister whose church is being used for the ceremony. This method of authorisation is, however, very rarely used.

Registrar

When, for whatever reason, the couple do not wish to marry in a church, the ceremony can take place under civil law in a register office or on approved premises. In England and Wales notice should be given to the local Superintendent Registrar (whose address can be found under 'Registration of Births, Deaths and Marriages' in the telephone directory), who will arrange the marriage in one of three ways:

1. By Superintendent Registrar's Certificate.
2. By Superintendent Registrar's Certificate and Licence.
3. By Registrar General's Licence.

With the exception of a licence issued by the Registrar General, notice may also be personally 'attested' before any local registrar of births and deaths or local registrar of marriages, but the notice is not held to have been duly given until it is received by the Superintendent Registrar and entered in his or her book.

1. ***Superintendent Registrar's Certificate:*** The official in this case will complete a form giving the names of the parties wishing to be

married, their residences and their ages. The form also requires mention of the building in which the marriage is to take place and concludes with a declaration, to be signed, which states that there is no legal objection to the marriage.

Both the man and the woman must have lived in the areas controlled by the registrars for seven days prior to giving notice. Only one of them need appear to make the declaration. If they live in different registration districts, either or both may make the declaration before the registrars and they must each have lived in their respective areas for seven days prior to the visit.

On being satisfied with the information supplied to him or her, the Superintendent Registrar will make the necessary entry in his or her notice book and, 21 days later, will issue the certificate for the marriage. The ceremony can then take place at any time within the three months following the entry in the notice book.

2. Superintendent Registrar's Certificate and Licence: For marriage by certificate and licence, a similar declaration must be made and signed as for a marriage by certificate, but the residential qualifications are different. Only one of the couple need give notice, even though they may live in different registration areas, provided that one of them has lived in the area for 15 days prior to the visit. However, the person not appearing must be within the borders of England and Wales or have his or her usual place of residence in England or Wales at the time notice is given.

One clear day after entering the notice, the Superintendent Registrar will issue the licence for the marriage (Sunday, Christmas Day and Good Friday are not counted). The licence is valid for three months following the date of entry in the notice book.

3. Registrar General's Licence: This method was introduced in 1970 and is reserved for cases of extreme illness where it would be impossible for the marriage to take place in a register office or other registered building. The licence permits the marriage to be solemnised in any place and at any time within three months from the date of entry in the notice book. There is no residence qualification and no statutory waiting period before the licence is issued.

Notice of marriage must be given (in person) by one of the couple to the local Superintendent Registrar.

Keeping on the Right Side of the Law

In addition to the formal procedures which have to be observed before any marriage can take place, there are a number of essential regulations concerning the conduct of the wedding ceremony itself and the freedom (in law) of the parties to marry.

a. With the exception of the Jewish and Quaker ceremonies, the special licence and a licence issued by the Registrar General, no wedding can take place before 8 a.m. or after 6 p.m.
b. A wedding cannot be private, hence the doors are not to be locked while the ceremony is proceeding.
c. Before the ceremony, all relevant certificates or licences must be produced and handed to the registering official.
d. Two persons must be present at the wedding, who will be required to sign their names as witnesses to the ceremony. They can be total strangers to each other and to the couple about to be married.
e. People under 16 years of age may not marry. In the case of a person over 16 but under 18, written consent to marry must be given by the parents (or parent) or other lawful guardians or guardian.

   If there is no parent or guardian to provide the necessary consent, application should be made to the courts for permission to marry. If it is felt that a parent or guardian's permission has been unreasonably refused, an application to overrule their decision can be made to the courts.
f. The marriage will not be valid if either party is already married.
g. Neither party to a divorce may remarry until the 'decree absolute' has been granted.
h. The parties must be respectively male and female by birth.
i. Both parties must be acting by consent and be of sufficiently sound mind to understand the nature of a marriage contract.
j. Marriages are forbidden between people who are closely related. Those relationships prohibited *by law* are listed on pages

23–24. Additional restrictions may apply when a marriage is to be performed according to the rites of some religious denominations.

Prohibited Degrees of Relationship

A man may not marry his:

mother, adoptive mother/former adoptive mother
daughter, adoptive daughter/former adoptive daughter
father's mother
mother's mother
son's daughter
daughter's daughter
sister
father's sister
mother's sister
wife's mother
wife's daughter
father's wife
son's wife
father's father's wife
mother's father's wife
wife's father's mother
wife's mother's mother
wife's son's daughter
wife's daughter's daughter
son's son's wife
daughter's son's wife
brother's daughter
sister's daughter

A woman may not marry her:

father, adoptive father/former adoptive father
son, adoptive son/former adoptive son
father's father
mother's father

son's son
daughter's son
brother
father's brother
mother's brother
husband's father
husband's son
mother's husband
daughter's husband
father's mother's husband
mother's mother's husband
husband's father's father
husband's mother's father
husband's son's son
husband's daughter's son
son's daughter's husband
daughter's daughter's husband
brother's son
sister's son

The Marriage (Prohibited Degrees of Relationship) Act 1986 (for England, Scotland and Wales, but not Northern Ireland) allows a man to marry his mother-in-law, step-mother, step-daughter or daughter-in-law without having to obtain a private Act of Parliament. By the same Act, a woman may marry her father-in-law, step-father, step-son or son-in-law. However, for marriages between in-laws, the former spouses must have died. Marriages under this Act are not permitted with the calling of banns, but can take place in church by licence or by a Superintendent Registrar's Certificate.

Any further information or clarification about whom you may or may not marry can be obtained from your local Superintendent Registrar.

FREE CHURCHES

The Order of Service used by the Free Churches (United Reformed, Baptist, Methodist and other Protestant bodies) is broadly similar to that of the Church of England. First of all, the chapel or building where the marriage is to take place must be registered for marriages and the registrar or other authorised person (usually the minister) must be present to register the marriage. In addition to the 'authorised person' the marriage must be witnessed by at least two people who have reached the age of 18.

Although there is considerable similarity to the Church of England, each of the denominations has its own Order of Marriage which should be read beforehand. Your local church or one of the following organisations should be able to provide further help and advice.

Baptist Union of Great Britain,
Baptist House,
129 Broadway,
Didcot,
Oxfordshire OX11 8RT   Tel: 01235 5120 77

Methodist Church Press Office,
Westminster Central Hall,
Storey's Gate Westminster,
London SW1H 9NH   Tel: 0171 222 8010

The United Reformed Church,
86 Tavistock Place,
London WC1H 9RT   Tel: 0171 916 2020

OTHER DENOMINATIONS

If the marriage is to be conducted according to the rites of a religious denomination other than the Church of England, notice of marriage must still be given to the authorised registrar for the area concerned, who will grant a licence.

The building where the marriage is to take place must normally be registered for marriages, except in the case of Jewish weddings (see page 26) and the registrar or other authorised person must be present to register the marriage.

Roman Catholic Ceremony

A Roman Catholic priest will require up to six months' notice of an intended wedding and longer if possible. This is regarded as an essential period of time for preparation, whether both parties are Catholic or not. If one party is a non-Catholic, there will be a different form of service.

Banns are required to be read out in the parish churches of both bride and groom, except when one of them is a non-Catholic, in which case no banns are read.

Jewish Ceremony

Civil law allows Jewish weddings to take place anywhere; in a synagogue, private house, hired hall or in the open air. They can also take place at any time except the Jewish Sabbath or festival or fast days.

Quaker Ceremony

If only one partner is a member of the Society of Friends the other will be asked to state that he/she is in sympathy with the nature of the marriage and also to provide two letters of recommendation from members of the Society. Their Registering Officer gives advice and information, then completes the required formalities for the wedding to proceed.

* * *

Your local religious body or one of the following organisations should be able to provide further help and advice:

Catholic Marriage Care,
Clitherow House,
1 Blythe Mews,
Blythe Road,
London W14 0NW Tel: 0171 371 1341

Jewish Marriage Council,
23 Ravenshurst Avenue,
London NW4 4EE Tel: 0181 203 6311

Religious Society of Friends (Quakers),
Friends' House,
173-177 Euston Road,
London NW1 2BJ Tel: 0171 387 3601

THE ROYAL NAVY

If one of the parties to the marriage is a serving member of the Royal Navy, the banns may be published aboard ship by the chaplain or commanding officer. In the case of a wedding in a register office or other registered building, the commanding officer may record the particulars in place of the registrar and issue the necessary certificate 21 days after notice has been given.

SCOTLAND

The law on marriage in Scotland is now governed by The Marriage (Scotland) Act 1977. The couple can be married by a registrar or assistant registrar, and the wedding will normally be held in their office. Alternatively, if they want a religious ceremony, they can be married by any member of the clergy, parson, priest or officer of any denomination who is entitled to undertake marriages under the Marriage (Scotland) Act. Whatever the type of wedding there must be two witnesses present who are at least 16 years of age.

In order to set the wedding wheels in motion, the couple must each get a marriage notice form from a registrar of births, marriages and deaths in Scotland. It does not matter which registrar is initially approached, but when the forms are filled in, they must be returned to the registrar for the district where the ceremony is to take place. Ideally, this should be done a month or more before the wedding date, and except in very exceptional circumstances a minimum of 15 days' notice must be given. If either party has been married before, the notice period is six weeks.

The marriage notice form is designed to establish whether the two parties are eligible to get married – for example, in terms of age, existing marital status and sex – and that they are not related to each other in any way which forbids marriage. They have to sign a declaration that the information given is true; if it is not, the marriage will not be valid.

When the marriage notice forms are returned, the registrar will also wish to see the relevant birth certificates. If either party has been widowed or married before, he or she will also need to produce a death certificate for their former spouse, or a copy of the divorce decree, remembering that a decree nisi from a court outside Scotland is not sufficient. If either party lives outside the United Kingdom, evidence is required to show that there is no legal reason in their own country why the marriage should not proceed. When producing any foreign documents, it is important to get a certified translation, and if there is any doubt about what is needed, the registrar should be consulted.

If there is delay in getting any of the required documents, it is best to return the marriage notice form anyway, explain the situation, and get the documents to the registrar as soon as possible.

The registrar will check the facts given on the marriage notice form and then prepare a marriage schedule. For a civil marriage they will keep the schedule in their office until the wedding, but for a religious ceremony it must be collected in person, not more than a week before the wedding. After the ceremony both parties sign the schedule, as do the two witnesses and whoever conducted the wedding. The schedule must be returned to the registrar within three days so that they can register the marriage.

As well as getting the marriage notice organised in good time, it is important to inform the person who will perform the ceremony of the preferred date. Particularly in towns, and at popular times of year, you will need to book early.

If one party lives in England or Wales but is marrying someone who lives in Scotland (or whose parents live in Scotland), and wants the wedding to be in Scotland, it is possible to give notice without actually going north of the border to do so. Notice must be given to the Superintendent Registrar of the district in England or Wales, and similar notice given in Scotland in the normal way.

Notices issued in England and Wales are valid in Scotland and vice versa, provided only one of the parties is resident in Scotland. However, marriage by licence in a register office in England or Wales is not possible in this case.

NORTHERN IRELAND

Church of Ireland

Marriage in the Church of Ireland may take place by means of:

1. Banns.
2. Licence.
3. Special Licence.
4. Certificate issued by a Registrar.

1. Banns: The banns may be read in the church where the ceremony is to take place if both partners are Protestant Episcopalians.

2. Licence: One or both partners must be Protestant Episcopalians and one must have spent 14 days immediately prior to the service in the district of the church where it is to take place.

A Church of Ireland licenser will issue the necessary licence after having received confirmation of the required seven days' residence in the district prior to service of notice of the proposed marriage. Copies of the notice will be sent to the places of worship which the parties attend, and seven days after service of notice on him the licenser may issue the licence.

The marriage must take place within three calendar months of the date of notice.

3. Special Licence: Provided one or both partners are Protestant Episcopalians, bishops may grant a special licence authorising the marriage to proceed at any time or place within their jurisdiction.

4. Registrar's Certificate: This authorises the marriage to take place in a church providing one or both of the partners are Protestant Episcopalians. If they live in different districts, separate applications must be made and the registrar must send a copy of the notice of marriage to the clergy of the places of worship attended by the partners and to the member of the clergy of the church where the marriage is to be solemnised if this is different. At least one of the partners must have lived for 15 days in the district of the church where the marriage is to take place.

The Roman Catholic Church

Marriage in the Roman Catholic Church may take place by:

1. Episcopal Licence.
2. Banns.
3. Licence.
4. Certificate issued by a Superintendent Registrar of Marriage.

1. Episcopal Licence and *2. Banns:* Both partners must be Roman Catholic and should apply to their parish priest or priests for information about the steps to be taken.

3. Licence: One or both partners must be Roman Catholic; where only one partner is Roman Catholic, notice in writing must be given to the person empowered to issue licences seven days before the licence shall be issued and that person must send copies of the notice to the clergy of the places of worship which the partners attend.

4. Registrar's Certificate: This may be obtained to authorise marriage in a Roman Catholic Church when one of the partners is not Roman Catholic.

Presbyterian Church in Ireland

Marriage in the Presbyterian Church in Ireland can be authorised by means of:

1. Banns.
2. Licence.
3. Special Licence.

1. Banns: The banns may be read in the church or churches of which the parties are members and the wedding must take place in one of these churches. Authorisation of marriage by this method is not permissible if the wedding is going to take place in the church of any other denomination or if one of the marriage partners is a member of another church body, even if that is another Presbyterian church such as the Church of Scotland.

2. Licence: Marriage by licence requires that one or both of the parties must be members of the Presbyterian Church in Ireland. Consent of parents or guardians must be obtained if one or both of the partners is under 18 years of age (21 in the Republic of Ireland) and this proviso applies to any of the three forms of authorisation.

When application is made to the minister they will issue a certificate confirming that one of the partners has been a member of the congregation for at least the past month. The certificate should be produced for a licensing minister. Allowing at least seven days' notice for granting the licence, it will subsequently need to be produced for the officiating minister before the marriage ceremony takes place.

The time restrictions imposed on this method of marriage are:

a. residential qualification of 15 days within the Presbyterian area immediately prior to the wedding;
b. the wedding must take place within three calendar months of the entry in the licensing minister's notice book;
c. the wedding must take place within one calendar month of the date of the licence.

3. Special Licence: Once again the requirement is membership of the Presbyterian Church in Ireland of one or both parties. The licence, which is issued by the Moderator of the General Assembly of the Presbyterian Church in Ireland, authorises the marriage to take place at any time or place in Ireland and is valid for three months. There is no residential requirement for either party.

* * *

Your local church or one of the following organisations should be able to provide further help and advice:

Catholic Marriage Care,
Clitherow House,
1 Blythe Mews,
Blythe Road,
London W14 0NW Tel: 0171 371 1341

Presbyterian Church in Ireland,
Church House,
Fisherwick Place,
Belfast BT1 6DW Tel: 0123 232 2284

The General Register Office for Northern Ireland,
Oxford House,
49-55 Chichester Street,
Belfast BT1 4HL Tel: 0123 225 0000

MARRIAGES OF BRITONS ABROAD AND FOREIGN NATIONALS IN THE UK

If marriage abroad is contemplated, first find out what documents (if any) will be required for the marriage to be legal. You will probably be asked to provide a certificate of no impediment to marriage, and your birth certificate, proof of residency, proof of no convictions etc. The extent of the requirements varies according to the regulations of each country. If you are still living in Britain, check with the foreign consul of the country concerned.

The marriage will generally be held to be legally valid under British law provided it is performed in accordance with the law of the country in which it takes place and that none of the regulations in British law regarding the relationship of the parties or their freedom to marry are contravened. The marriage must also be monogamous. However, the situation varies according to individual circumstances and final judgement may rest on a court decision.

On the other hand, marriage under British law is not necessarily valid in every foreign country, so if a foreign national wishes to marry in the United Kingdom, he or she should consult their consul or other representative in Britain to ensure that the contemplated marriage ceremony will be accepted as legally binding in their own country. This applies whether the marriage is to a British subject or to someone of their own nationality.

THE CHURCH AND DIVORCE

In the *Church of England* clergy have the legal right to refuse to marry in church anyone whose previous partner is still alive. However, they will probably be prepared to conduct a Service of Blessing at some time after the civil ceremony has been performed. Despite the Church's general ruling on this matter, some ministers may still offer to perform the full wedding service.

The *Church of Scotland* will allow a church ceremony if either party has been married before, provided that the couple comply with the required notice period of six weeks. Banns will not be read in church as this requirement was abolished by the Marriage (Scotland) Act 1977.

Civil divorce is not recognised by the *Roman Catholic Church*. If a divorced person was contemplating remarriage it would have to be established that the first marriage was not recognised by the Roman Catholic Church. This would mean either that a declaration of nullity had been granted by a Roman Catholic Marriage Tribunal or that a previous marriage had not complied with Church Law.

Civil remarriage in England and Wales is allowed if the divorced person can produce a decree absolute. Remarriage in a register office can then proceed in exactly the same way as a first marriage. The decree absolute is obtainable on application by the successful petitioner six weeks after the decree nisi which first pronounced the divorce.

Civil remarriage in Scotland is possible directly after the divorce is announced, because in Scotland there is no equivalent to the decree nisi; the decree is absolute immediately.

CHANGING YOUR NAME

A woman does not have to change her name when she gets married, although it is generally expected and usually makes life a little easier when making joint social, legal or financial arrangements.

Sometimes a woman retains her maiden name for professional purposes, if changing it would be inconvenient or potentially damaging. Having two separate identities is confusing, but it may be the best solution in some circumstances.

If you do decide to change your name, however, there are lots of people who will want to know about it. It may take a little time to get round all the relevant authorities and organisations, but here are some of the more important ones to note:

> Employer, bank, building society, savings accounts, insurance companies, credit card companies, passport office (you don't have to change the name on your passport, but it is usually more convenient if you do), Inland Revenue, Department of Health and Social Security, DVLC (for change of driver's licence and vehicle registration documents), your doctor and your dentist.

If you are going abroad on honeymoon, you will require a passport. The issue of family passports with particulars of husband and wife included has been discontinued. If you wish to travel abroad in your married name, collect the relevant forms from the Post Office for the issue of a post-dated passport. New applicants and those who wish to have existing passports amended will also need to complete the relevant forms.

Completed application forms should be sent to the Passport Office for your particular area. These are listed on the application form and you should allow at least one month for the application to be processed and up to three months if applying between February and June.

CHECKLIST: CHURCH OF ENGLAND

- [ ] Both parties must be over 16
- [ ] If under 18, obtain parents' consent
- [ ] For divorced people, obtain a decree absolute and agreement of the minister
- [ ] Choose church
- [ ] Apply to minister of church
- [ ] Arrange for publication of banns
- [ ] Ask minister of church to publish banns
- [ ] If one partner living in different parish, also arrange for banns to be called in that parish

Banns to be read out during morning service on:

- [ ] 1. ....
- [ ] 2. ....
- [ ] 3. ....
- [ ] Attend calling of banns
- [ ] **OR** Obtain a common licence
    - [ ] If one partner living in parish for preceding 15 days, he/she can apply in person
    - [ ] Obtain licence

OR Obtain a special licence ☐

- Apply to the Archbishop of Canterbury ☐
- Provide sworn statement of reasons special licence required ☐
- Obtain licence ☐

OR Obtain Superintendent Registrar's Certificate ☐

- If one partner living in district for preceding seven days, he/she can apply in person ☐
- Notice entered ☐
- Obtain certificate (after 21 days) ☐

Finalise date of ceremony............................ ☐

Finalise place of ceremony .... ☐

CHECKLIST: THE REGISTER OFFICE/APPROVED PREMISES

- [ ] Both parties must be over 16
- [ ] If under 18, obtain parents' consent
- [ ] For divorced people, obtain a decree absolute
- [ ] Provide details of names, ages, addresses etc.
- [ ] Provide evidence that there are no legal reasons why the marriage should not take place, such as death certificate of former spouse or decree absolute
- [ ] Choose register office/approved premises
- [ ] Obtain Superintendent Registrar's Certificate
    - [ ] If both living in district for preceding seven days, one partner can apply in person
    - [ ] If living in different districts for preceding seven days, one partner may apply in person to respective Superintendent Registrars
    - [ ] Notice entered in Superintendent Registrar's notice book
    - [ ] Obtain certificate (after 21 days)
- [ ] **OR** Obtain Superintendent Registrar's Certificate and Licence
    - [ ] If one partner living in district for preceding 15 days, he/she can apply in person

Other partner living in England or Wales at time notice given ☐

Notice entered in Superintendent Registrar's notice book ☐

Obtain certificate (after one clear day) ☐

OR Obtain Registrar General's Licence ☐

Apply in person to Superintendent Registrar ☐

Obtain licence ☐

Finalise date of ceremony .... ☐

Finalise place of ceremony .... ☐

CHECKLIST: SCOTLAND

- [ ] Both parties must be 16 or over
- [ ] Obtain marriage notice forms
- [ ] Return marriage notice forms with birth certificates, and death certificate or divorce decree certificate if second marriage
- [ ] Collect marriage schedule
- [ ] Finalise date of ceremony ....
- [ ] Finalise place of ceremony ....
- [ ] Sign marriage schedule and arrange for it to be signed by two witnesses and person who conducted the wedding
- [ ] Return marriage schedule to registrar within three days

3

THE WEDDING PREPARATIONS

The announcement of your engagement is the first step in the process of getting married and marks the beginning of much careful planning and preparation for the wedding day itself.

THE TIME AND PLACE

Once you have decided on the form of ceremony you would like and when it is to take place, you should go to see the minister or registrar concerned so that the proper religious and/or legal arrangements can be made.

At the same time ensure that a suitable venue for the reception will be available on the day you have chosen; in fact, it is often necessary to book the reception before the church. After all, the church can accommodate a number of weddings on one day, but the hall or hotel is probably available for just one.

If you are going to be married in church you should discuss with the minister the details of the ceremony including the style and order of service, whether or not a choir should be present, the music to be played and the possibility of bell-ringing. Also find out about the fees (there are basic legal statutory fees, but other church costs are at the discretion of the minister), and ask if your guests will be allowed to take photos in the church and throw confetti in the church grounds. The minister will want to talk to you about the significance of a church wedding and may invite you to attend a marriage preparation course which takes a broad look at all the issues involved.

In all aspects of the marriage ceremony the minister is the expert and their advice and guidance will be well worth having.

If you have decided on a civil ceremony, however, you should go to see the local Superintendent Registrar as soon as possible. Apart from the legal formalities, you should find out how many guests can be accommodated at the ceremony, particularly if it is to be held in a register office, and whether photographs and confetti are allowed.

Most people who decide to get married in this way do so because they are divorced, want a quiet ceremony with no fuss, or because a marriage in church would conflict with their own beliefs.

LETTERS OF ANNOUNCEMENT

If there are people whom the couple would particularly like informed about their forthcoming marriage, but because of the limitations of the guest list they have not been able to invite them to the wedding, a personal letter is probably the best way to let them know the news.

PERSONAL LETTERS OF INVITATION

Before the formal invitations are sent, relatives and close friends may be informed by personal letter, the wording for which could be:

> 'You will be glad to hear that Patricia and Robert's wedding has been arranged for 27 April. We shall, of course, be sending you a formal invitation later, but we felt sure you would be delighted to have the news as soon as possible.'

INVITATIONS

Invitations are traditionally from and sent out by the bride's parents as they generally host the occasion (indicating their responsibility for payment of the reception), but if the wedding is being hosted by anyone else, such as the bride and groom themselves, they should take on this task.

The invitations should be sent out well in advance of the date set for the wedding; six to eight weeks is about right. They should be sent out simultaneously, as prospective guests do not like to assume that they are second choice!

The list of guests is usually drawn up by the bride and her mother in consultation with the bridegroom and his parents. The engagement list will serve as a useful guide, although there are sure to be some omissions and additions. Although the best man and attendants will already have been consulted they must also receive invitations to which they should reply formally and promptly. Similarly, the groom's parents should also receive an official invitation. It is courteous to invite the minister to the reception.

The invitations are normally composed in the third person and sent from the bride's parents. Traditionally the invitation is addressed to the wife of the couple or family. The wording on the invitation of those invited can be formal (Mr and Mrs Alan Smith) or less formal (Alan and Ruth Smith) or informal (Alan and Ruth) depending on the formality of the wedding and the relationship with those invited. If there is to be a disco or dance after the reception this should be included, with an indication of suitable dress, in the bottom right-hand corner of the invitation.

The bride's surname is not normally included but it can be appropriate if it differs from that of the host and hostess. The most popular wording is:

Mr and Mrs David Smith
request the pleasure of
the company of

....
(write the name of the guest(s))

at the marriage of their daughter
Patricia
to
Mr Robert Brown
at All Saints' Church
Kingsgrove
on Saturday, 27 April
at 2.45 p.m.
and afterwards at a reception at
The Bell Inn, Kingsgrove

RSVP
21 Firhill Lane
Kingsgrove
Kent

For those guests who are being invited to the reception only, you will need evening cards with wording such as:

Mr and Mrs David Smith
request the pleasure of
the company of

....

at an Evening Reception
to be held at
The Bell Inn, Kingsgrove
on Saturday, 27 April
at 7 p.m.
to celebrate the marriage of their daughter
Patricia
to Robert Brown

RSVP
21 Firhill Lane
Kingsgrove
Kent

If the number of guests is quite small, the invitations may be written by hand on suitable and attractive stationery. More often, however, they are printed. Visit a stationer's and have a look at the range of cards and styles of lettering that are available. Black is the traditional colour for the lettering. If you want to order reply cards, order-of-service sheets or cake boxes, you can do this at the same time.

When two daughters of the same couple are to be married at the same ceremony, the elder daughter of the two brides is mentioned first.

In the case of a daughter and a niece or god-daughter, the daughter is mentioned first as she is closest in relationship to the host and hostess.

Where two couples are themselves acting as hosts and hostesses, the elder couple is mentioned first.

If the occasion is a second wedding for one or both of the partners – especially after divorce – it is likely to be a much less formal affair. The bride and groom will probably host the wedding and send out invitations with less formal wording such as:

Patricia Smith and Robert Brown invite you to their wedding at All Saints' Church, Kingsgrove, on Saturday, 27 April at 2.45 p.m. and afterwards to a reception at The Bell Inn, Kingsgrove.

In the unfortunate event of a family bereavement or severe illness you will probably want to postpone the wedding, and notices will have to be sent to all those invited to attend. A plain statement of the facts is quite sufficient, with notice of the new date for the wedding, if one has been arranged:

Owing to the recent death (illness) of Mr David Smith, the wedding between Patricia Smith and Mr Robert Brown at All Saints' Church, Kingsgrove, at 2.45 p.m. on Saturday, 27 April, has been postponed to 4 p.m. on Friday, 30 May.

Formal replies to invitations should be sent promptly (within three days of receiving the invitation) and are also traditionally drawn up in the third person. The following is the usual wording:

Mr and Mrs John Clemence thank Mr and Mrs David Smith for their kind invitation to their daughter's wedding and to the reception and will be most happy to attend.

However, when the guests are very close friends of the host and hostess, a brief, informal thank-you note is acceptable.

WEDDING PRESENTS

Traditionally, relatives send a gift whether or not they attend on the day. Guests attending the ceremony and the reception are expected to donate a gift. A friend need not give a gift if the invitation has been declined and there is no need to send a gift if invited to the ceremony only. Gifts should be sent to the bride at her parents' home before the wedding; if sent afterwards, they should be addressed to both the bride and groom at their home. It is good manners to invite gift donors to the ceremony and usually, though not necessarily, to the reception.

It should be remembered that a wedding guest has no obligation to send the bridal couple a wedding gift, nor should the bride's mother feel that every gift donor should be 'rewarded' with an invitation to the wedding. In practice, however, most guests do send a gift and most donors do get invited to the wedding party. It is in order to send the gift as soon as news of the impending wedding is received.

The business of giving or receiving wedding presents is always a little daunting – to both sides. Visions of dozens of toasters and electric kettles loom before the eyes of the engaged couple, while the guests are naturally concerned that their carefully chosen gifts should be received with the proper appreciation.

Even the best-laid plans go wrong sometimes, but there are some practical steps you can take to ensure that this particular wedding custom turns out happily (as far as possible) for all concerned.

There are really only two rules for the bride to remember:

1. Have a wedding-present list prepared for anyone who wishes to consult it. You should, of course, wait to be asked to submit the list rather than send it automatically with invitations or other wedding correspondence.
2. Be sure to write thank-you letters to everyone who sends you a present.

1. The Wedding List

Once you have compiled a list of the presents that you would like, you should make a number of copies and let people have one when they ask. Ask them, when they have bought their present, to return the list with the item they have bought crossed off. The list can then be handed to somebody else. Although this method is not guaranteed to avoid duplication it is probably bettered only by employing the services of a large store: you compile your list from the items in the store, guests then ring the store, make their purchase and the store adjusts the list. This method has obvious drawbacks but may be worth considering.

The list itself should contain a good number of inexpensive as well as expensive presents, and should run to more items than you actually expect to receive. This avoids the possibility of the last guest to see the list being left to buy the colour television set!

Traditionally, bed linen for the bridal couple's new home was given by her parents as part of the bride's trousseau. Traditional gifts for the home such as linen, china, glass, cutlery and home accessories are still popular as both the bride and groom benefit, but for the couple who already have these items less traditional gifts are acceptable, if they can be enjoyed by both partners. More expensive gifts such as carpets and furniture are usually reserved for very close relatives or groups of friends banding together to share the cost.

There is, however, no reason why you should think only in terms of fitting out the home. Books, pocket calculators, compact discs or sports equipment may be more useful to you and more urgently required. So do consider what your real needs are before finally drawing up the list.

It used to be considered bad form for anyone other than close family to give money, but today this is not the case. When writing to say thank you it is polite to say how the money will be spent.

It is traditional for members of the wedding party to exchange lasting mementos. The bride and groom exchange gifts, the bride's parents give a gift to the groom, the groom's parents give a gift to the bride, and the groom gives a gift to the best man, the ushers, the bridesmaids and page boys. The bride and groom give a gift to their mothers.

2. Thank-you Letters

Although you can, if you like, ignore the need for a wedding list and perhaps even survive the resultant chaos, the same cannot be said of the need to write thank-you letters. It is so obviously discourteous and hurtful not to thank people who sent you presents that you should be especially careful not to leave anyone out. Whenever possible gifts should be delivered well before the date of the wedding itself and thank-you letters sent personally and promptly, making mention of the gift and something complimentary about its appearance and usefulness.

A methodical approach to the letters is the only answer. Whenever you receive a present, make a note of what it is, who sent it and when it arrived. Write to the person concerned as soon as possible, thanking them for the gift and put a tick against their name when the letter is in the post.

This task traditionally falls to the bride, but if the bridegroom has received any personal gifts, he should reply himself.

Displaying the Presents

It is natural for the guests to want to see the wedding presents, and a display may be arranged at the reception or in the bride's parents' home. There are certain risks involved, however. If the display is to be at an outside reception, perhaps at a big hotel, there may be a chance of some petty thieving from uninvited 'guests'. Moreover, you will be effectively advertising the contents of your future home to anyone who happens to be in the vicinity.

For that reason, it is usually safer to stage the display at a private house. The only snag is that some guests feel embarrassed to see their own relatively inexpensive presents ranged against other more valuable items. It will help if you dispense with the usual custom of using name tags to accompany the presents; if cheques have been received, you should set out cards stating simply 'cheque from ...' without divulging the amounts. The same applies to a display set up at the reception.

THE ENGAGEMENT RING

The giving of an engagement ring is an ancient custom; it is the token of the pledge the couple make and announces to others that the woman's affections are already engaged. It is always worn on the third finger of the left hand. It used to be the practice for the man to present the girl with an engagement ring if she accepted his proposal; today, as mentioned earlier, most couples choose the ring together.

THE WEDDING RING

The act of giving a wedding ring or the exchange of rings is at the heart of the church marriage service and is a part of its ritual and tradition. The wedding ring does not have to be a new one; it can be a family heirloom, an old or antique ring. Wearing the wedding ring before the ceremony is considered unlucky and there is a superstition which says it is unlucky to buy engagement and wedding rings on the same day. Even so, when buying the wedding ring it is a good idea to see if it looks well alongside the engagement ring.

You can follow fashion when choosing the wedding ring, but often a simple, traditional style proves to be the best choice, never looking old-fashioned even after many years.

It is not necessary for the bride to give the groom a gift, but a ring or some other item of jewellery often forms part of the ceremony these days.

DRESSING FOR THE OCCASION

The Bride's Dress

For a church wedding, the traditional dress is white with a train; the dress covers the bride from neck to wrists and ankles, though it may have a see-through net area from collar to bust. A veil is traditionally worn for modesty. There is no ecclesiastical objection to women marrying in trousers but most ministers (and brides) probably prefer to see a dress. Older and second-time brides are entitled to wear white if they wish, though cream is a more usual choice.

It is a custom that the bride's dress is kept a secret before the wedding for good luck.

Choosing a wedding dress that will look and feel absolutely right on the day is one of the most important (and enjoyable) decisions the bride must make during the run-up to the ceremony. The long wedding gown is still very popular and many brides marrying in a register office or on approved premises choose a traditional wedding dress, though probably without a train or long veil. White is still the main choice of colour, even for some brides who are pregnant or when the bride and bridegroom have been living together before the wedding.

Wedding dresses can be hired, bought ready made or professionally made for you by a dressmaker. Alternatively, a close friend or relation may offer you the use of her wedding dress. This may be a very good proposition if the style suits you and if any necessary alterations are minimal.

The eventual choice will largely depend on the significance you attach to the dress itself and the sort of wedding you want. You may opt for a traditional white silk or lace dress with head dress and veil, or choose a different colour such as cream or oyster, or a patterned dress.

Whichever kind of dress you choose, give yourself plenty of time to look around and try on different examples. You should also allow time for the dress to be altered, if necessary, or made, if you are having one specially designed.

Outfits for Women Attendants

A matron of honour is a married woman attendant; a maid of honour is an unmarried woman attendant. If there is a matron or maid of honour as well as bridesmaids, she will not wear the same dress as the younger attendants.

Dresses for the Bridesmaids

It used to be the bride's privilege to dictate entirely the style of dress worn by her bridesmaids and it was traditional that she or her family paid for them. Today they have a say in the matter and most bridesmaids at least contribute to the cost.

After consulting the bridesmaids, the bride chooses their dresses (and the pages' outfits), the main criteria being that they should complement her own wedding outfit. A dramatic contrast in colour, for example, will do little to enhance the bridal procession – or the wedding photographs. It might also look a little odd if the bride appeared in a plain dress while the bridesmaids were adorned with frills and lace. Bear in mind, too, that bridesmaids vary in size, shape and colouring. You are trying to find something to suit them all, so avoid too much finery, or colours that are too strident.

Outfits for the Mothers of the Bride and Groom

In order to avoid disappointment and embarrassment, the mothers should liaise. The bride's mother has first choice.

Male Outfits

Male members of the wedding party include the bridegroom, the best man, the ushers and both fathers, all of whom should dress with the same degree of formality. When the bride wears white traditionally the groom should wear morning dress, and other male members of the wedding party should follow suit. Theoretically, all male guests ought to do likewise, although in practice it is usually only the immediate members of the family who wear this costume.

Generally, morning suits are either all grey, or consist of a black tail coat and pinstripe trousers. They look good in the wedding photographs with traditional accessories such as hats and gloves, although these can be rather a nuisance with more time spent carrying them and getting them mixed up than actually wearing them. The groom and his party are not actually required to wear their top hats, although morning dress is considered incorrect and incomplete unless hats are carried.

Morning suits may be hired or bought off the peg, or you could have one tailor-made. For the majority, however, hiring a suit will be the best answer. Remember that the summer months are the most popular for weddings and formal social functions, so reserve your suit well in advance.

The favourite alternative for most weddings is a well-cut two- or three-piece lounge suit, which will form a welcome addition to the wardrobe after the great event. The principal men should take their cue from the bridegroom when deciding what to wear; they should not outshine him on the big day.

Clothes for Guests

The invitation wording should indicate correct dress. A reception after 6 p.m. can mean evening dress. 'Black tie' means that men wear a black dinner jacket and bow tie; women wear long or evening dress.

The rule that all women in church wear hats has been relaxed, but because of tradition most will like to do so. Similarly, the convention that only those women guests who are in deep family mourning should wear black is no longer observed.

Outfits for Double Weddings

The whole bridal party should dress with the same degree of formality.

THE FLOWERS

Flowers are a very important part of every church wedding. Usually there will be bouquets or posies for the bride and bridesmaids and buttonholes for the principal men, and the church and reception area will be decorated with displays. There may also be sprays and corsages for the two mothers, and the bride may wish to wear a head-dress of fresh flowers or attach just one flower to her hair or veil.

At one time it was considered obligatory for brides to carry white bouquets, but now almost anything goes. A fairly large bouquet suits a formal long dress with a train; a neat posy complements a shorter dress. Bouquets are traditionally carried by the bride and bridesmaids.

Buttonholes are usually worn by the principal men of the wedding party who normally wear white carnations. The groom, best man and fathers sometimes have double red carnations; ushers usually have single red or white buttonholes. The men's buttonhole flowers are worn on the left.

The bouquets can be chosen from a selection of designs suggested by the florist, who will also be the best person to ask about suitable flowers for the church and reception.

If the arranging is not to be carried out professionally, the flowers may still need to be ordered several weeks in advance of the ceremony, especially if the preference is for unusual or out-of-season flowers. They should not be collected until one or two days before the wedding, when the larger displays are arranged. The bouquets, buttonholes and other dress flowers are usually delivered or collected on the morning of the wedding and the dress flowers are distributed at the church before the ceremony.

It will be necessary to get the permission of the minister to decorate the church, so arrange a time when this can be conveniently carried out. He or she may be able to suggest someone who can help in return for a small donation.

It may also be possible to combine with other couples who are getting married in the church on the same day; the minister should be able to supply names and addresses.

When choosing the flowers, remember to take into account the character and size of the church and reception areas. A large, formal display, for example, would look out of place in a small room or a country church. It is also a good idea to have a theme – of colours and/or varieties – running through from the bride's bouquet to the flowers used in the church and reception. As with the wedding dresses, aim for a sympathetic blend of colour and form.

If the wedding is to take place in a register office, it may already be decorated with flowers. Check with the Superintendent Registrar. If not, you may be able to arrange for a simple display to be set up before the ceremony.

If the wedding is to take place on approved premises, the proprietor may include the provision of flowers for the register room and reception. Check with them. If not, again you may be able to organise your own displays.

THE PHOTOGRAPHS

Your wedding day will be one of the most memorable days of your life, so it is imperative that you have a beautiful set of photographs to remind you of it.

A professional photographer should be your first choice and you may find that some acquaintance who has recently married can recommend one. Otherwise try looking in the windows of local photographers and see if you can pinpoint anything in the display of their work that attracts you. Ask to see further examples of work and start comparing possible costs.

You will need to agree with the photographer beforehand any specific photographs that you would like to be taken before, during or after the ceremony. Check with the minister or with the proprietor of the approved premises as to whether he or she imposes restrictions on photography inside the church or register office/ room.

In addition to the official photographer, relatives and friends will want to take photographs, but they must not be allowed to interfere with the work of the official photographer. The best man or an usher should politely advise guests.

If the photography is entrusted to an amateur, he or she should be reimbursed for the cost of the film.

VIDEOS

If you are contemplating video coverage of your wedding, you will have to make enquiries of a number of people who offer this service. It may be financially advantageous to use the same firm to take both the still photographs and the video. Once again you will need the minister's or registrar's approval, since the video team may need to visit the church or approved premises to test not only for lighting, but for angles and sound.

THE PRESS

Even if the engagement has not been announced in a newspaper, many couples like to insert a notice (or send a card) giving the time and place of the forthcoming wedding, to appear a few days before the date, so that any casual friends and acquaintances may, if they wish, join in wishing them well at the church, register office or approved premises. Suitable wording would be:

Mr and Mrs David Smith
are pleased to announce
the marriage of their daughter
Patricia to Mr Robert Brown
at 2.45 p.m. on Saturday, 27 April
at All Saints' Church, Kingsgrove.
All friends welcome at the church.

Newspapers usually have their own style for entries, so check in the selected one for suitable wording.

The newspaper may also publish an account of the wedding, sometimes by sending a reporter/photographer, but more often by issuing a standard form to be filled in and returned with a photograph after the wedding.

CHECKLIST: SUGGESTED WEDDING LIST

Many of these ideas can be divided into several specific suggestions, for example, glasses can be divided into the various types you would like. You may wish to specify particular colours or styles you would prefer for many items. You will also need to consider the more personal gifts you would like to add.

Kitchen
Baking tins and trays
Coffee percolator/cafetiere
Cookery book
Crockery
Cruet set
Cutlery
Deep fat fryer
Dishwasher
Food processor
Freezer
Kettle
Kitchen linen
Kitchen tools
Knives
Microwave
Oven
Pedal bin
Pressure cooker
Salad bowls
Sandwich toaster
Saucepans
Scales
Storage jars and tins
Toaster
Trays
Tumble dryer
Washing machine
Wok

Dining room
Decanters
Dinner service
Glassware
Table and chairs
Table linen
Wine corker
Wine rack

Sitting room
Bookcase
Furniture
Magazine rack
Standard lamp
Stereo
Table lamp
TV
Video recorder

Bedroom
Bed
Bed linen
Electric blanket
Furniture
Lamp
Mirror
Radio alarm

Bathroom
Bath mat
Bathroom cabinet
Bath towels
Hand towels
Flannels
Mirror
Paper holder
Scales
Toothbrush holder
Towel rail
Waste bin

Garage, Garden and DIY
Barbecue set
Drill
Garden furniture
Garden tools
Lawn mower
Tool box
Tools
Washing line
Workbench

Miscellaneous
Candlesticks
Cushions
Clocks
Luggage set
Ornaments
Photo album
Radio
Rugs
Smoke detector
Sports equipment
Vases

CHECKLIST: THE PHOTOGRAPHS/VIDEO

- Select and book photographer ☐
- Select and book video team (if different) ☐
- Obtain minister's/registrar's approval for ceremony video ☐
- Arrange programme of sequential items for video ☐

Photographs may be requested of:

- Bride's dressing table ☐
- Before leaving for the wedding ☐
- Leaving the house ☐
- The best man and groom before the ceremony ☐
- Arriving at the church/register room ☐
- Inside the church (with minister's permission)/register room ☐
- Signing the register (with minister's permission) ☐
- Leaving the church/register room ☐
- Bride and groom ☐
- Couple with parents ☐
- Couple with best man, bridesmaids and pages ☐

- Couple with bride's family ☐
- Couple with groom's family ☐
- Couple with friends ☐
- Bridesmaids and pages ☐
- At the reception ☐
- Cutting the cake ☐

Discuss any special effects required, e.g. couple in wine glass ☐

Arrange for proof photographs to be made available at the reception ☐

Take orders for photographs from family and guests ☐

Give order to photographer ☐

Distribute photographs ☐

4

THE PRINCIPAL PLAYERS

In this chapter we look at the duties of the principal players at a traditional English wedding. We have based the timetable of events primarily on a Church of England wedding, but the duties involved still apply to a large extent on whether the wedding is in church, chapel, register office or approved premises and for many other faiths, including Roman Catholic and some Free Churches, although it cannot be applied to foreign nationals marrying in this country or to weddings of members of the Jewish and Quaker faiths.

The marriage ceremony occurs continuously around the country throughout the year. Naturally it becomes more popular during the summer months, especially June, which is named after the goddess Juno, the adored and faithful wife of Jupiter, who is the protector of women and marriage. Juno is said to bestow special blessings on those who wed in her month:

> Married in the month of roses – June
> Life will be one long honeymoon.

Guests who attend weddings, turning up on the wedding day in their best outfits and bearing gifts, have little occasion to think of the preparations that have been under way for many months, and the role of the principal players who will ensure that everything goes smoothly.

There are just half a dozen of these principal players, all playing their part, large or small, and invariably everybody goes away saying what a grand day it was, and didn't the bride look lovely.

The bride is, of course, the undoubted star. It is her day. She is going to be the centre of attention for the entire day; even the groom has a secondary role, and the other players form a supporting cast.

THE BRIDE

Every bride wants to look her best on her wedding day, when she will be the centre of attention for the bridegroom and all the guests, and the feature of wedding photographs and videos.

Duties

Invariably the bride's main concern will be her wedding dress, but there are many other things that she and her mother will need to organise before the big day such as: appointing attendants (chief bridesmaid, bridesmaids and page boys); compiling the guest list; drawing up the guest/gift list and writing thank-you letters; arranging press announcements; compiling a budget; booking the ceremony and reception; ordering the cake; booking the photographer and/or video maker team; booking transport; booking the florist; arranging the 'hen night'.

The bride's main function on this, her special day, is to look beautiful. She will have the assistance of her mother and the chief bridesmaid when she is getting ready. Then, with her father or whoever is giving her away, she leaves for the church, making sure that she does not arrive early.

At the church entrance the chief bridesmaid will arrange the bride's dress, veil and train. The bride then takes her father's right arm and proceeds slowly down the aisle to where the bridegroom and best man are waiting. She then hands her bouquet to the chief bridesmaid so her hands are free for the ring to be put on. At the end of the marriage service, the bride accompanies the groom in the procession to the vestry to sign the register. The bride and groom then lead the procession out of church with the bride on the left arm of her husband.

After the photographs have been taken outside the church, the bride and groom are the first to leave for the reception, where they will shortly be joined by the bride's parents and the groom's parents. Together they form a welcoming line for the arriving guests.

At the end of the meal come the toasts and speeches, and though the bridegroom speaks on behalf of his bride and himself, the bride may wish to say a few words of her own.

At some time the bride throws her bouquet to the waiting bridesmaids, the tradition being that the one who catches it will be the next to marry. Sometimes, of course, the eager, outstretched hands belong to some of the young, unmarried guests! The moment for this ritual is either when the bride is going upstairs to change into her going-away outfit or when she is getting into the car, ready to leave in a shower of confetti.

Expenditure

Traditionally the bride's family pays for the reception; the bride's dress and attendants' outfits; transport for the bride, her father, her mother and the bridesmaids to the church, and for the bride's father and mother and bridesmaids to the reception; flowers for the church and reception; stationery; gift to the groom; hen night.

Families nowadays are more likely to make alternative financial arrangements for some of the major expenses, so although traditionally the bride's father pays for her wedding dress, she may decide that she will pay for her own dress or alternatively for the bridesmaids' dresses.

THE BRIDEGROOM

As mentioned earlier, the bridegroom has only a supporting role on the day. If his earlier decision in the choice of best man was a good one, then he will have saved himself some anxious moments on the day, as a good best man can do a great deal to help the groom throughout the day.

Duties

The groom will liaise with the bride and her mother on most issues concerning the wedding arrangements. He is directly responsible for obtaining the necessary legal documentation by applying to the minister or registrar; choosing and advising his best man; organising outfits for the principal men; organising the honeymoon; acquiring a wedding ring; organising transport to and from the church and transport from the reception in liaison with his best man; paying for flowers for the bride and attendants, for the buttonholes and sprays; preparing and delivering a speech.

Before the wedding day the groom will decide, probably with the help of his bride-to-be, what the male dress will be. If his choice is morning suit, then the best man, ushers and fathers of the bride and groom will be required to follow suit.

As the wedding draws near many of the groom's male friends and colleagues will be keen to know when and where the stag party will be held. It is advisable, for everybody's sake – and especially the groom's – to have the celebration at least two days before the wedding, so that any after-effects have time to wear off!

The groom will have the best man in attendance on the morning of the wedding, lending him moral support and making sure he gets to the church about 20 minutes before the ceremony is due to start. Before they set off for the church the groom can give the best man the wedding ring and the wedding documents. He may also want the best man to look after other items such as tickets and passports and possibly car keys. If the bride and groom are changing into going-away clothes at the reception, the groom should have these ready to give to the best man.

Having arrived early at the church, the groom now has to endure a waiting and wondering period until the bride's arrival. After the service he accompanies the bride in the procession to the vestry to sign the register. The couple then lead the procession out of church with the bride on the left arm of her husband.

After the photographs have been taken outside the church, the bride and groom are the first to leave for the reception, where they will shortly be joined by the bride's parents and the groom's parents. Together they form a welcoming line for the arriving guests. The recognised order is:

the bride's mother and father
the groom's mother and father
the bride and groom

The bridegroom will be called upon to reply to the toast made by the bride's father and will speak on behalf of his bride and himself. Some information on the subject of speeches will be found towards the end of this chapter.

Expenditure

The bridegroom's expenditure starts with the engagement ring. Today he is not expected to stand the entire cost of the stag party; everybody present pays a share. Naturally he will pay for his own outfit, whether bought or hired, and if hired he might also pay for the best man's and ushers'. He may wish to buy the best man and other attendants a small gift each as a memento of the occasion.

The bridegroom also pays church or registrar's expenses; he should hand the money to the best man on the wedding morning so he may pay the member of the clergy or verger.

Naturally the groom will pay for his bride's wedding ring and her bouquet, together with those of the bridesmaids; he will also pay for buttonholes for himself and all the principal men, and for sprays for the two mothers. He will also pay for the car to take him and the best man to the church and the car to transport him and his bride to and from the reception.

Last, but by no means least, he will pay for the honeymoon.

THE BEST MAN

In the majority of cases the best man will be either a close friend or relative of the bridegroom. His main function is to look after the groom and to lend his assistance generally to see that the big day goes without a hitch. Together, the bridegroom and best man choose the ushers, whose main role will be to show the wedding guests to their seats in the church, hand out service sheets or prayer books and help the best man make sure that everyone has transport to the reception.

Duties

The best man's main task, of course, is to get the bridegroom to the church on time, but before the wedding day itself he has several important jobs which must not be neglected. Traditionally he has to make sure that everything is in order regarding the groom's clothes, both for the wedding and his going-away clothes. The best man may be entrusted with these and have to take them to the reception if the newlyweds are leaving for their honeymoon directly from there. He may also be asked to look after the bride's suitcase. If suits are being hired it is likely that the bridegroom and best man will go to the hire shop together; if the bridegroom is in a magnanimous mood he may foot the bill for the best man's and ushers' outfits, but the best man and ushers pay for their own suits if they are not hired.

The best man's other major pre-wedding day job is to organise the stag party which, from the men's point of view, of course, is a very important event. The best man should ensure that it is not held on the eve of the wedding, just in case there are any celebratory after-effects.

On the morning of the big day, if order-of-service sheets have been printed, he has to collect them from the bride's mother and get them to the church, or perhaps delegate the job to an usher. Buttonholes for himself, the groom and the ushers could probably be collected at the same time, together with any telemessages or cards for the couple.

He then sets off for the groom's house where he will take charge of any documents, such as tickets, passports, wedding documents and, of course, the ring.

Having made sure that the groom is looking his best, the best man should get him to the church about 20 minutes before the service is due to start. During the service the best man's prime function is to produce the ring or rings at the appropriate moment. After the service he will accompany the chief bridesmaid in the procession to the vestry for the signing of the register and may be called upon to sign as a witness.

After the photographs are done, the best man has to arrange transport to the reception for all the guests. Alternatively, he may entrust this task to the ushers and accompany the bridesmaids to the reception. If the bride and groom are leaving the reception by car, the best man may have the additional task of parking the car nearby and looking after the keys.

At the reception, the best man requests silence for grace, makes a short speech, reads out a selection of telemessages and cards and tells the guests the rest of the programme for the reception. Some information on speeches will be found towards the end of this chapter.

If the suits were hired for the wedding the best man will no doubt have to return the bridegroom's, together with his own and possibly those of the ushers.

Expenditure

Apart from buying himself a new suit or hiring an outfit and purchasing a wedding gift for the bride and groom, the best man's expenses are relatively light. The bridegroom will provide him with the money to pay any wedding fees and any other incidental expenses.

THE BRIDESMAIDS AND PAGES

The choice of bridesmaids and pages can sometimes pose problems for the bride, not only in the number of attendants, but their respective ages. Whatever the final choice, the selection of chief bridesmaid will no doubt be decided quite early on in the proceedings. She will probably be a sister or close friend of the bride. If she is already married herself, her title is matron of honour, but her duties remain the same.

Duties of Chief Bridesmaid (or Matron of Honour)

Her initial task might be to assist the bride in her choice of wedding dress and perhaps help decide on the bridesmaids' dresses. She will assist the bride as much as possible with the wedding planning and preparations.

On the wedding day she will go to the bride's house in the

morning and help her with her preparations: dressing, make-up, hair etc. She can also help any younger bridesmaids to dress and give them some last-minute instructions. The bridesmaids and pages then proceed to the church and wait at the entrance.

When the bride arrives at the church, the chief bridesmaid will arrange the bride's dress, veil and train, then follow her in procession down the aisle. She will probably then be handed the bride's bouquet for the duration of the ceremony.

After the service she will accompany the best man in the procession to the vestry for the signing of the register and may be called upon to sign as a witness. She can then return the bride's bouquet to her and, once again accompanied by the best man, follow the bride and groom from the church.

At the reception she has no specific duties, though she might assist the bride in her going-away preparations, take charge of young attendants and help to display and record gifts received.

Expenditure

Traditionally the bride pays for the bridesmaids' outfits, particularly if they are unlikely to be worn again.

The Pages

Page boys are usually between five and eight years old and make a beautiful picture with the bride. The bride arranges for their outfits. They follow the chief bridesmaid up the aisle, wait at the chancel steps and follow the chief bridesmaid and best man out of the church. They leave for the reception with the chief bridesmaid and the best man (if he does not remain behind) and hand out slices of cake at the reception.

Expenditure

As for bridesmaids, the bride generally pays for their outfits.

THE USHERS

The ushers are the best man's helpers. They are traditionally unmarried and are usually brothers or close relatives of the bride and groom.

Duties

The ushers escort the bridesmaids during the course of the day and instruct guests about rules regarding photography and confetti.

They should arrive at the church early, three-quarters of an hour before the service is due to start. They are required to distribute buttonholes, greet people at the church entrance, ascertain whether they are guests of the bride or groom, then show them to their seats, handing them order-of-service sheets or prayer books at the same time. Bride's guests are seated on the left of the aisle and the groom's on the right, although if there is an extreme imbalance it is permitted to discreetly even out the numbers. The front pews are for close family. The groom's parents sit in the second pew from the front.

After the ceremony the ushers help the best man to ensure that everyone has transport to the reception. At the reception the ushers help to make the event enjoyable by looking after the guests.

Expenditure

Ushers arrange and usually pay for their own outfits if they can be worn again, but if hired, the groom generally pays.

THE BRIDE'S MOTHER

The bride's mother takes no official part in the ceremony, yet to all intents and purposes she organises the wedding every step of the way.

Duties

The whole thing starts for her with the organisation of the guest list and sending out the invitations. Bearing in mind that she and her husband are footing the bill for many of the wedding day costs, she has to compile a guest list which is fairly balanced for both bride and groom. In fact there are often two lists: one for the wedding service followed by the reception and another for guests invited to the reception only.

Booking the hall or hotel for the reception may be done by her or alternatively by the bride and groom. She will also order the wedding cake, or perhaps even make it herself, arrange for the printing of order-of-service sheets and order wedding cars for the bride and her father, the bridesmaids and, of course, herself and any other guests who require transport from her house to the church. Then she must organise the flowers: buttonholes for the guests, bouquets and decorations for the church and reception. Although the bridegroom traditionally pays for the buttonholes and bouquets for the principal players, it is better if they are all ordered together to maintain a theme of colours or varieties. She will also need to book the photographer and make the catering arrangements for the reception if it is being held in a hall rather than a hotel.

These are just the major items; there are a thousand and one other minor problems to solve and she must ensure that not too many of them cause last-minute panics which might upset the arrangements on her daughter's big day.

On the morning of the wedding, she will help her daughter get ready and attend to all the last-minute details as well as getting herself ready. If the reception is to be held at home she will have considerably more to do in preparing for the returning guests.

She travels to the church with the bridesmaids to arrive before the bride. She is the last one of the 'guests' to enter the church and is escorted to her seat by the chief usher. She sits in the front pew on the left of the aisle.

At the close of the service she joins the bridegroom's father as the wedding party proceeds to the vestry for the signing of the register. She comes out of the church, still with the bridegroom's father, then after the photographs outside the church rejoins her husband. They should be the first, after the newlyweds, to leave for the reception, where they will be first in line to greet the guests as they arrive.

She and her husband, together with the best man, are the last to leave the reception. After the reception, she is responsible for sending slices of cake to those unable to attend and organising the photograph proofs.

THE BRIDE'S FATHER

Although traditionally the bride's mother organises the wedding, no doubt she will be assisted in many ways by her husband, since there is a considerable amount of preparation involved and decisions to be made. Many couples may share the organisation.

Duties

On the subject of dress the bride's father complies with the bridegroom. If the groom decides that the order of dress will be morning suits, then all the male attendants are required to dress in the same way, including the bride's father and the bridegroom's father.

The main duty of the bride's father is to give his daughter away on her wedding day. When she is ready to leave the house, he accompanies her to the church, then escorts her down the aisle. At the appropriate time in the service, when the minister asks who is giving the bride away, he will take his daughter's right hand and place it in the hand of the minister.

When the service is over he will join the bridegroom's mother as the wedding party proceeds to the vestry for the signing of the register. He also accompanies her out of church, then rejoins his wife.

Once the newlyweds have departed, the bride's parents need to be the next to leave the church to be ready to greet the guests at the reception.

The next duty of the bride's father is to say grace if there is no minister present. He makes a short speech after the meal. Some information on speechmaking appears towards the end of this chapter. The bride's father and mother are the last to leave the reception.

Expenditure

When it comes to wedding costs, it might be easier to list the items that the bride's father (or in reality, these days, the bride's parents) does not pay for, as traditionally he pays for almost everything on the occasion of his daughter's wedding. Very often nowadays, however, the groom or the groom's father will offer to contribute some part of the cost. The bride's father's main expense will probably be the reception and this is often the area where the bridegroom's father offers to share the cost.

The first bill for the bride's father may be for the engagement party. Then he will have the cost of printing invitations and order-of-service sheets, followed by the bride's dress and attendants' outfits, wedding cake, flowers for the church and reception, cars and photographer.

He will probably buy a new suit or hire morning dress, his wife will have a new outfit, and there will be many other small incidental expenses.

Older couples and those who have lived together generally pay for the wedding themselves. It would be inappropriate to expect retired parents to take on the financial responsibility.

TOASTS AND SPEECHES

Something which many dread and renders others totally dumb is speechmaking. The thought of standing up and 'saying a few words' fills many hearts with fear. If you feel that 'the speech' is a major obstacle, a copy of *Wedding Speeches and Toasts* by Barbara Jeffery, *Wedding Speeches* by Lee Jarvis or *Mitch Murray's One-Liners for Weddings* will prove to be a great help. Apart from guidance on writing and presenting speeches, there are specimens that you can use or adapt as your own.

Order and Content of Speeches

Toasts and speeches are generally made at the end of the wedding breakfast and it may well fall to the best man to act as toastmaster.

1. The bride's father will be called upon first. It is traditional for the bride's father to propose the toast to the bride and groom, but if the bride's mother is a widow the toast should be made by a relative of mature years (an uncle, for example, or an old family friend). Specific content of the speech obviously depends on the relationship of the speaker to the bride, but a speech made by the bride's father will normally include the following main points:

    a. how proud he and his wife are of their daughter;
    b. a welcome to his new son-in-law, with perhaps the old saw about gaining a son not losing a daughter;
    c. a welcome to the bridegroom's parents;
    d. words of wisdom and good wishes to the newlyweds;
    e. how confident he and his wife are that the couple's future together will be happy;
    f. a toast to the bride and bridegroom.

2. The bridegroom will reply on behalf of his bride and himself along the following lines:

    a. thanking his father-in-law for his comments;
    b. thanking the bride's parents for giving him their daughter in marriage and for the wedding;
    c. thanking his own parents for what they have done;
    d. thanking the guests for coming and for their gifts;
    e. saying how wonderful his bride is, and how fortunate he is;
    f. acknowledging the invaluable help given by his best man;
    g. thanking all helpers who have made the day a success;
    h. expressing regret if a close family member or a close friend is unavoidably absent;
    i. proposing a toast to the bridesmaids.

He may make presentations of the gifts to the attendants if he has not already done so.

3. The best man replies on behalf of the bridesmaids, expressing:

    a. the thanks of the bridesmaids for the toast, adding a few complimentary remarks of his own;
    b. the thanks of the bridesmaids for their presents;
    c. how lucky the groom is to have won such a bride;
    d. what a good chap he is anyway and it is what he deserves;
    e. congratulatory wishes from a selection of telemessages and cards received;
    f. the programme for the rest of the reception.

It is acceptable to group together those telemessages and cards which bear the same or similar good wishes and read the sentiment once only, adding the names of the senders.

The points given are very general ones. It is advisable for speechmakers to find out early on what aspects they will be expected to cover in their speeches, and if there are any awkward areas (e.g. family feuds, divorce or separation in the family etc.) that should be avoided.

Jokes are acceptable provided they are not 'blue' or likely to offend any guests. Aim to speak for a maximum of five minutes; you will be surprised how long five minutes can be when you are standing in front of an audience!

After the three traditional speeches other guests may wish to say a few words; perhaps the bridegroom's father and sometimes the bride. It is essential that the best man or toastmaster ascertains beforehand whether there are likely to be any other speakers so that he can call upon them before the guests relax, thinking that the speeches have finished.

The toast to the bride and groom at a bride's second marriage may still be proposed by the bride's father, but this is unusual; he is not after all giving his daughter away in marriage this time. It would more likely be proposed by a male friend. There are normally only two speeches – this one and the groom's response.

How to Say It

Once you have a draft of your speech prepared to approximately the right length, keep it with you so you can look at it from time to time, and update it as you gain any new information that you wish to include. Do not try to learn it by heart. Instead, get thoroughly familiar with it, so that you can speak it naturally, glancing at your 'script' from time to time to refresh your memory. You will need to speak a little more slowly and distinctly than normal, but never shout and, if you have a regional accent, do not try to change it.

Rehearsing in front of a mirror, taping your voice as you speak, can be very useful in boosting your self-confidence. A video of your speech will be helpful in assessing your performance and will highlight any irritating habits you are unaware of, which might annoy the guests.

Points to Remember:

- Prepare your speech well beforehand. Compile it in large writing, in dark ink, or print clearly. It is useful to highlight pauses and paragraph starts in colour so you can see these at a glance.
- Keep it short. Five minutes is maximum.
- Do not include 'blue' jokes.
- Do not refer to the honeymoon, any previous marriage or liaisons, future family or sex.
- Try not to repeat yourself or over-use the same words or phrases.
- Make sure you have your speech with you when you arrive at the reception.
- Do not drink too much before you present your speech.
- Go to the lavatory in good time before making your speech.

- Speak a little more slowly and clearly than normal, and do not forget to breathe!

- Do not deviate from your prepared speech. You could end up saying something you regret.

CHECKLIST: THE BRIDE

Preparations (*with the bridegroom; **with the bride's mother)

Discuss with minister*: ☐

- Church decorations ☐
- Music ☐
- Organist ☐
- Choir ☐
- Bells ☐
- Order of service ☐
- Fees ☐
- Confetti ☐
- Photographs in church ☐
- Video in church ☐

Choose chief bridesmaid/matron of honour ☐

Choose bridesmaids ☐

Choose pages ☐

Draw up guest list** ☐

Arrange for wedding dress and accessories ☐

- Buy ☐
- Make ☐
- Hire ☐

- Arrange for outfits for bridesmaids and pages ☐
  - Buy ☐
  - Make ☐
  - Hire ☐
- Book hairdressing appointment ☐
- Order wedding cake and arrange for delivery** ☐
- Order bouquets for self and bridesmaids and arrange for delivery** ☐
- Order sprays for bride's and groom's mothers, and buttonholes for bridegroom, bride's and groom's fathers, best man and ushers, and arrange for delivery** ☐
- Select and book photographer** ☐
- Order wedding cars for wedding party to church and to reception** ☐
- Write wedding present list ☐
- Choose wedding breakfast menu** ☐
- Choose wines** ☐
- Arrange press announcement** ☐
- Choose going-away outfit and luggage ☐
- Write thank-you letters for presents as they arrive ☐
- Pack for honeymoon ☐
- Attend rehearsal ☐

On the day

- Give gifts to bridesmaids ☐

- [ ] Take luggage and going-away outfit to reception

At the church

- [ ] Arrive last on father's right arm and proceed up the aisle followed by bridesmaids
- [ ] At chancel steps give bouquet and gloves to chief bridesmaid
- [ ] Allow chief bridesmaid to lift veil
- [ ] After service, with bridegroom follow minister to sign register
- [ ] Leave church with bridegroom
- [ ] After photographs, leave first with bridegroom for reception

At the reception

- [ ] Greet guests with bridegroom after parents
- [ ] With groom, cut cake
- [ ] After reception, change into going-away outfit
- [ ] Save flower from bouquet, and toss bouquet on leaving

CHECKLIST: THE BRIDEGROOM

Preparations (*with bride)

Arrange for registrar or clergy* ☐

Choose best man ☐

Choose ushers ☐

Buy wedding ring* ☐

Arrange and pay for wedding outfit ☐

- Buy ☐
- Hire ☐

Plan, book and pay for honeymoon ☐

Organise and pay for stag party ☐

Arrange and pay for car from reception ☐

Buy bridesmaids' gifts ☐

Buy best man's gift ☐

Write speech for reception ☐

Pay for:

- Flowers of bride and attendants ☐
- Buttonholes and sprays ☐
- Car for self and best man to church ☐
- Car for bride and self to reception ☐

Choose going-away outfit and luggage ☐

Pack for honeymoon ☐

Attend rehearsal ☐

On the day

Give gift to best man ☐

Give money to best man for church fees ☐

Take luggage and going-away outfit to reception ☐

Take going-away car to reception ☐

At the church

Arrive with best man at ....o'clock ☐

Step up to altar when bride arrives ☐

After service, with bride follow minister to sign register ☐

Leave church with bride ☐

After photographs, leave first with bride for reception ☐

At the reception

Greet guests with bride after parents ☐

Respond to toast 'The bride and groom', give speech and propose toast to 'The bridesmaids' ☐

With bride, cut cake ☐

After reception, change into going-away outfit ☐

Collect documents etc. from best man ☐

CHECKLIST: THE BEST MAN

Preparations

Send formally written reply to invitation within three days of its receipt ☐

Discuss wedding plans with bride, groom and chief bridesmaid ☐

Help to choose ushers ☐

Arrange for own outfit ☐

Buy ☐

Hire ☐

Check that groom and ushers have organised their outfits ☐

Explain duties to ushers ☐

Write speech for reception and check with bride about specific people to be mentioned ☐

Help to organise stag party ☐

Check parking facilities at church and reception ☐

Purchase wedding present and car decorations ☐

Check groom has all necessary documents for wedding and honeymoon ☐

Arrange for car to take groom and self to church ☐

Note details of emergency taxi firms ☐

Check routes to groom's home, to church and to the reception venue ☐

Attend rehearsal ☐

On the day

- [ ] Check that bridegroom's luggage is ready
- [ ] Check that bridegroom's change of clothes is ready
- [ ] Arrange for going-away car to be parked at reception and keep keys
- [ ] Have tickets and documents for honeymoon
- [ ] Have cash for church fees
- [ ] Keep wedding rings safe
- [ ] Have documents for wedding
- [ ] Collect buttonholes from bride's mother and take to church
- [ ] Collect telemessages, cards and order-of-service sheets from bride's mother
- [ ] Collect bridegroom at .... o'clock and take to church

At the church

- [ ] Ensure that ushers know duties
- [ ] Hand order-of-service sheets to ushers
- [ ] Make sure bridegroom, groom's father, self and ushers have buttonholes, and bride's and groom's mothers have sprays
- [ ] Pay fees to minister
- [ ] Wait on right of groom and hand over ring or rings at appropriate time
- [ ] After service, with chief bridesmaid follow bride and groom to sign register
- [ ] Take charge of groom's hat and gloves in church

- Leave church with chief bridesmaid ☐
- Usher couple and principal parties to places for photographs ☐
- Make sure ushers have arranged transport for guests to reception ☐
- After photographs, see couple to car to take them to reception ☐
- Leave for reception with bridesmaids after bride and groom, or wait till last ☐

At the reception

- Join the end of the receiving line or take charge of guests' coats ☐
- Offer drinks to guests ☐
- Take charge of any late wedding presents ☐
- Collect and vet telemessages and cards ☐
- Guide guests to seating plan ☐
- Request silence for grace ☐
- Call on speakers if there is no toastmaster ☐
- Respond to toast of 'The bridesmaids', give speech, read telemessages and cards, give programme for rest of reception ☐
- Place luggage in car for honeymoon ☐
- Oversee decoration of the going-away car ☐
- Hand over documents, keys etc. for the honeymoon ☐
- See couple to car after reception ☐
- Take charge of groom's wedding outfit ☐

After the wedding

- Return wedding outfits of groom and self if hired ☐

CHECKLIST: THE USHERS

Preparations

Arrange for own outfits ☐

Buy ☐

Hire ☐

At the church

Arrive at the church at ....o' clock ☐

Collect order-of-service sheets from g best man ☐

Conduct guests to their pews and hand out order-of-service sheets ☐

Ensure guests have transport to reception ☐

At the reception

Offer drinks to guests ☐

After the wedding

Return outfits if hired ☐

CHECKLIST: THE CHIEF BRIDESMAID (MATRON OF HONOUR)

Preparations

- [ ] Arrange for own outfit
- [ ] Attend rehearsal

On the day

- [ ] Help to dress the bride for the ceremony
- [ ] Make sure bouquets are ready for bride and bridesmaids
- [ ] Look after bridesmaids and pages

At the church

- [ ] Assemble with bridesmaids and pages in church porch
- [ ] Arrange bride's dress, veil and train for procession up the aisle
- [ ] Take bride's bouquet and gloves at chancel steps
- [ ] Lift bride's veil
- [ ] After service, with best man follow bride andgroom to sign register
- [ ] Return bouquet and gloves to bride in vestry
- [ ] Leave church with best man after bride and groom
- [ ] After photographs, leave for reception with best man and other bridesmaids, after bride and groom

At the reception

- [ ] Offer drinks to guests
- [ ] Check that bride's going-away outfit is ready
- [ ] Check that bride's luggage is ready
- [ ] Help bride change into going-away clothes
- [ ] See bride to car

After the wedding

- [ ] Return bride's and own outfit if hired

CHECKLIST: THE BRIDE'S MOTHER

Preparations (**with bride)

Draw up guest list** ☐

Arrange printing of invitations ☐

Arrange printing of order-of-service cards ☐

Send invitations ☐

List acceptances received ☐

Draw up final guest list ☐

Prepare seating plan ☐

Arrange wedding outfit ☐

Buy ☐

Make ☐

Order bouquets for bride and bridesmaids and arrange for delivery** ☐

Order sprays for self and groom's mother, and buttonholes for bridegroom, bride's and groom's fathers, best man and ushers, and arrange for delivery** ☐

Arrange church decorations ☐

Select and book photographer** ☐

Make arrangements for reception at.................... ☐

Home ☐

Hotel ☐

Restaurant ☐

Private hall ☐

- Make catering arrangements ☐
  - Self ☐
  - Professional caterers ☐
- Choose wedding breakfast menu** ☐
- Choose wines** ☐
- Arrange for table decorations ☐
- Arrange accommodation for guests ☐
- Arrange for printed napkins ☐
- Arrange for printed place setting cards ☐
- Arrange for musicians/entertainment ☐
- Order wedding cars for wedding party to church and to reception ☐
- Order wedding cake and arrange for delivery** ☐
- Buy wedding cake boxes ☐
- Arrange for neighbour to lock house after bride and father have left ☐
- Attend rehearsal ☐

At the church

- Arrive before the bride at ....o' clock ☐
- After service, with groom's father follow bride's father and groom's mother to sign register ☐
- Leave church with groom's father ☐
- After photographs, leave for reception with husband after bridesmaids ☐

At the reception

- [ ] With bride's father, greet guests
- [ ] When all guests have arrived, give signal for wedding breakfast to begin
- [ ] Arrange display of gifts
- [ ] Arrange changing room for bride
- [ ] Arrange display of proof photographs
- [ ] Take orders for photographs from family and guests

After the wedding

- [ ] Send pieces of cake to relatives/friends who could not attend wedding
- [ ] Give order to photographer
- [ ] Collect and distribute photographs

CHECKLIST: THE BRIDE'S FATHER

Preparations

Arrange for wedding outfit ☐

- Buy ☐
- Hire ☐

Write speech for reception ☐

Pay for (usually shared with wife):

- Reception ☐
- Flowers to decorate church and reception ☐
- Wedding dress ☐
- Wedding cake ☐
- Photographer ☐
- Wedding cars ☐
- Press announcement ☐
- Hairdressing ☐
- Invitations and order-of-service printing ☐

Keep buttonhole at home when other sprays/ buttonholes taken to church ☐

Attend rehearsal ☐

At the church

Arrive last with bride on right arm and proceed up aisle ☐

At appropriate moment, give bride's right hand to minister ☐

- After service, with groom's mother follow best man and chief bridesmaid to sign register ☐
- Leave church with groom's mother ☐
- After photographs, leave for reception with wife after bridesmaids ☐

At the reception

- With bride's mother greet guests ☐
- Say grace if there is no minister present ☐
- When called by best man, give speech and propose toast to bride and groom ☐
- Wait until all guests have departed before leaving the reception ☐

5

THE MARRIAGE CEREMONY

Before the ceremony itself takes place, there will almost certainly be an opportunity to attend a rehearsal in the church. The minister will run through all the details of the service and explain the roles of each of the principal members of the wedding party.

It is best if the whole wedding party can attend the rehearsal, but if that is not possible it will help if the best man can be present so that he can later advise anyone who is unsure of the correct procedures.

CHURCH OF ENGLAND WEDDINGS

If you are getting married in an Anglican church, you should have already discussed with the minister whether the service is to be traditional or if it is to be conducted according to an Alternative Service Book version. The minister may have his or her own very definite opinions about this, but both ceremonies are very moving.

If the parents of either the bride or the bridegroom are divorced, a little tact and co-operation all round will help to ensure that the wedding is still a happy occasion, both for them, and for the couple about to be married.

In these circumstances the seating arrangements at the church are slightly altered. If the bride's parents are divorced, her mother will be shown to the first pew on the left-hand side of the church. She may be with her new husband, or, if she has not remarried, with a close relative. The bride's father takes his seat in the second or third pew, also with his new partner if he has remarried. The same arrangements apply to the bridegroom's parents if they are divorced.

Twenty minutes or so before a Church of England wedding is due to begin, the guests will start to arrive. The bride's family and friends are conducted to the left-hand seats of the church and the bridegroom's family and friends to those on the right. The bridegroom and the best man are seated in the front pew on the right-hand side. The bride's mother usually travels to the church with the bridesmaids, who remain in the church porch until the bride and her father arrive.

When the bride has taken her place at the church entrance, the organist will play the entrance music. At this point the congregation rises. The bride takes her father's right arm and they walk down the aisle followed by the bridesmaids. If it is a full choral service the minister may meet the bride in the porch and the procession will be led by the choir, followed by the minister, the bride and her father and the bridesmaids.

The bridegroom and the best man meet the party at the chancel steps. The bride stands on the left of the bridegroom, and her father to her left, but slightly to the rear. The best man positions himself on the right of the bridegroom and, like the father, slightly to the rear. (After the bride's father has given away his daughter, he can take his seat next to his wife in the front pew. The best man can also step to one side after he has presented the ring.)

At this point the chief bridesmaid steps forward to take the bride's bouquet or, if there are no bridesmaids, it may be handed to her father, who in turn may give it to his wife. The bouquet should be returned to the bride before she leaves the church, usually at the signing of the register.

The ceremony then begins. The minister first explains the significance of marriage according to the Scriptures. He or she then calls on the congregation – and the bride and bridegroom – to declare if there is any reason why the couple may not lawfully marry.

The minister then asks each of the couple in turn whether they promise to love, comfort, honour and forsaking all others (in the modern version) protect the other ... 'as long as you both shall live', to which they reply 'I will'.

The bridegroom takes the bride's right hand in his, and they exchange vows 'to have and to hold, from this day forward; for better, for worse, for richer, for poorer, in sickness and in health, to love and to cherish till death us do part'.

The best man gives the ring to the minister, and the bridegroom places it on the third finger of the bride's left hand, or sometimes rings are exchanged. The bridegroom then makes his promise to the bride as follows (in the modern version):

> 'I give you this ring
> as a sign of our marriage.
> With my body I honour you,
> all that I am I give to you,
> and all that I have I share with you,
> within the love of God,
> Father, Son and Holy Spirit.'

The bride responds with the same promise, beginning 'I receive this ring ...' and the minister then pronounces them man and wife. After the marriage, and before signing the register, the minister will sometimes give a short address, especially if one or both of the married couple are known to him or her.

When the service is ended, the wedding party move into the vestry to sign the register. The best man and the chief bridesmaid usually act as the two witnesses. Everyone has a chance to relax now, and one or two photographs are usually taken at the signing.

Coming out of the church, the bride takes the left arm of the bridegroom; they are followed by any small bridesmaids; the chief bridesmaid and the best man; the bride's mother and the bridegroom's father; the bridegroom's mother and the bride's father; and other bridesmaids, often escorted by the ushers. Relatives leave next, followed by special guests and then friends.

Outside, there will be a good deal of milling around as the wedding photographs are taken. Confetti (if it is permitted) will most likely be thrown when the bride and bridegroom decide it is time to leave for the reception.

PLACES DURING THE CHURCH OF ENGLAND CEREMONY

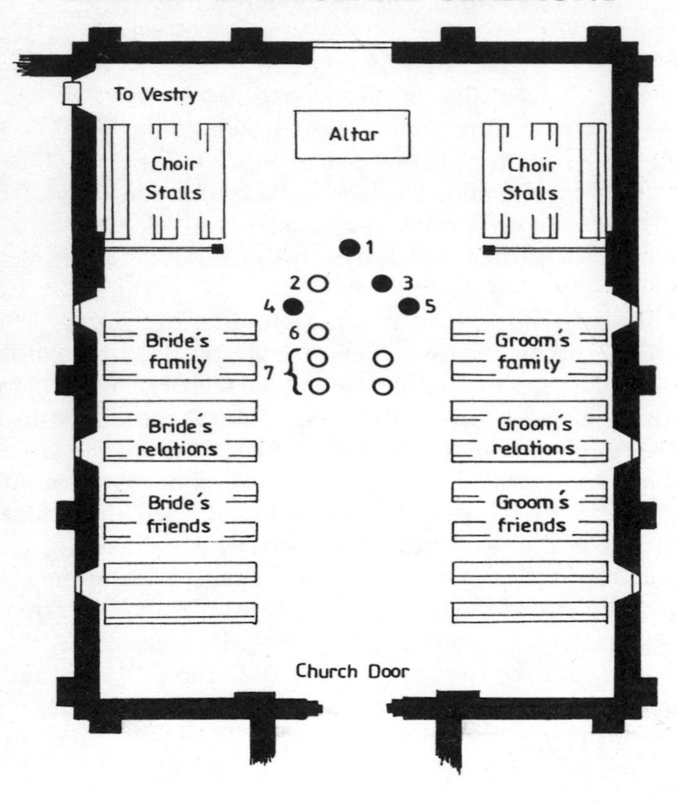

THE PROCESSION TO THE VESTRY AFTER THE CHURCH OF ENGLAND CEREMONY

Wedding Etiquette

THE PROCESSION TO THE VESTRY AFTER THE CHURCH OF ENGLAND CEREMONY

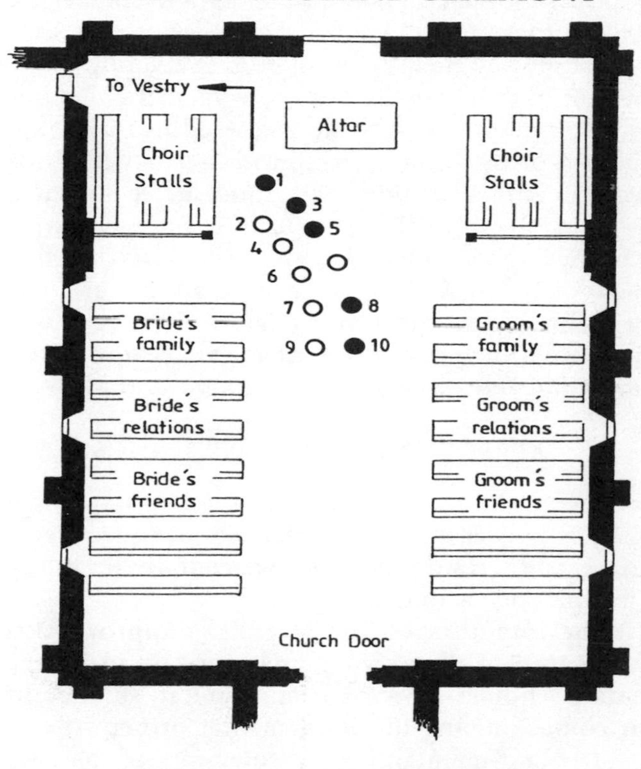

1. Minister
2. Bride
3. Bridegroom
4. Chief bridesmaid
5. Best man
6. Bridesmaids
7. Bride's mother
8. Groom's father
9. Groom's mother
10. Bride's father

REGISTER OFFICE WEDDINGS

The reasons that couples opt for a register office wedding are various, not least of them, of course, being financial. The cost of a full-scale church wedding is now said to average more than £6,000 (at 1998 prices). No matter how that sort of cost is shared, many couples obviously feel that there is a strong case in favour of a register office wedding.

Because there are generally size limitations in a register office there will be room for only a small number of guests to accompany the couple and their two witnesses. Everybody should arrive about ten minutes before the ceremony to ensure that it starts on time, as there will probably be another wedding following shortly. The tradition of the bride arriving with her father is not always followed; sometimes the bride and groom arrive together.

The ceremony takes about ten to 15 minutes and will be conducted by the Superintendent Registrar. The couple must state that they know of no legal impediment to marrying and will be reminded of the solemn and binding nature of the vows which they will repeat after the registrar. The ring or rings are exchanged and the relevant documents signed by the couple and the witnesses.

APPROVED PREMISES WEDDINGS

The Marriage Act 1994 changed the law in two ways; firstly, local authorities may license 'suitable premises' for the solemnisation of marriage, and secondly there is no need to live in the district in which the marriage is to take place.

It is the intention of The Marriage (Approved Premises) Regulations 1995 to allow civil marriages to take place regularly in hotels, stately homes, civic halls and similar 'suitable premises' without compromising the fundamental principles of English marriage law and maintaining the solemnity of the occasion. A private residential house is unlikely to be an appropriate building as it would not be known to the public as a marriage venue or regularly be available for use. The Regulations preclude marriages from taking place in the open air, in a marquee or any other temporary structure or in most forms of transport. A directory of registered premises in England and Wales is kept by the Marriages Section, P.O.Box 2, Southport, Merseyside, PR8 2JD (telephone 01704 569824).

Couples who choose approved premises generally have the ceremony at the reception venue, since this is much more convenient for the wedding party and guests.

The setting must not resemble a church in any way; for example, prayer books would probably not be allowed. The marriage room must be separate from any other activity on the premises and accessible to the public without charge so that they may witness the marriage and be able to make any objections. No food or drink may be sold or consumed in the marriage room for one hour before or during the ceremony.

As for a register office, the ceremony must not include any religious elements. Any reading, words, music or performance which forms part of a civil ceremony of marriage must be secular. Many Superintendent Registrars insist on confining the ceremony to include only the legal elements, with perhaps one or two very minor additions, and conduct the proceedings in registered premises rooms in the same way as they do in register offices.

On arrival at the approved premises, the Superintendent Registrar meets the couple privately to explain the procedure. Meanwhile guests gather in the marriage room. The Superintendent Registrar, the bride and groom then enter and the ceremony takes place. After the register is signed and the ceremony is ended, the Superintendent Registrar leaves the premises.

FREE CHURCH WEDDINGS

Most of the Free Church buildings have been registered by a Superintendent of Marriages as buildings in which marriages may be solemnised. Ministers of these churches, be they United Reformed, Baptist, Methodist or other Protestant churches, are generally registered as 'authorised' persons to conduct the marriage service and to act as the registrar, which simply means keeping the marriage register. If such authorisation has not been obtained, a Superintendent Registrar or his or her deputy must be present to record the wedding, although the minister may still conduct the ceremony. Alternatively, a civil ceremony may be conducted by the Superintendent Registrar in his or her office.

The order of service is very similar to that used in the Church of England, with variations within the different denominations. After the bridal procession arrives in front of the minister, together with the bridegroom and best man, the service begins with a declaration of intent. The bride and groom in turn will say:

> 'I do solemnly declare that I know not of any lawful impediment why I ..... may not be joined in matrimony to .....'

After the minister has asked the congregation if they know of any lawful objection to the marriage, the couple exchange vows and proceed with the ceremony of the ring followed by the blessing. After the service the newlyweds and two witnesses sign the register.

The question of remarriage of divorced people is very much a matter for each minister considering each case on its merits. He or she may have very strong views on the subject or may be willing to give careful consideration to the matter and agree to conduct a church service.

ROMAN CATHOLIC WEDDINGS

As with all marriages outside the Church of England, the couple must give notice of their intention to marry to the local

Superintendent Registrar (or registrars if they live in different districts). Often the priest or one of his parishioners will be authorised to register the marriage, in which case the registrar is not required to be present at the wedding.

The marriage ceremony may be conducted during Mass (called a Nuptial Mass) or outside Mass, usually when one of the couple is not a Roman Catholic. However, the rite of marriage is the same in either case.

The priest first addresses the bride and bridegroom on the significance of marriage within the Church: it is regarded as a sacrament which will 'enrich and strengthen' them so that the union will be one of 'mutual and lasting fidelity'.

The couple have to declare no lawful impediment to marriage; they promise to be faithful to each other and to accept that they bring up children within the Roman Catholic faith. The priest invites them to declare their consent to marry 'according to the rite of our Holy Mother the Church', to which each replies 'I will'.

Right hands joined, the couple then call upon the congregation to witness the marriage, and make their vows: 'to have and to hold from this day forward ... till death do us part'.

The priest confirms them in marriage and the rings are blessed and exchanged – or only one may be given – using the following words:

> 'I (Christian name only) take this ring as a
> sign of my love and fidelity. In the name
> of the Father and of the Son and of the
> Holy Spirit.'

JEWISH WEDDINGS

When Jewish people marry, they are required to give notice to the registrar, but the marriage may be solemnised in a synagogue or private house. When a synagogue or house is used, the secretary of the synagogue to which the man belongs must take down the necessary particulars.

The ceremony, when held in a synagogue, varies in the form it takes. The bride and bridegroom stand under a canopy – a *chuppah*

– which is a reminder of the time when the Israelites were forced to live in tents. The couple's parents join in the ceremony by standing under the canopy with them and supporting them. Behind are their relations and friends. The best man stands behind and to the left of the bridegroom.

The rabbi delivers a short address to the couple. Then the bridegroom turns to the bride, who stands to his right, and before placing the ring on her finger, says, 'Behold, thou art consecrated unto me by this ring, according to the law of Moses and of Israel.' The bride should wear no other rings or jewellery, not even her engagement ring.

The next step is the reading and signing of the Hebrew marriage contract. The man promises to be a true and faithful husband, and to protect, support, love, honour and cherish his bride. She promises to be true and faithful and to love, honour and cherish him.

Following the vows, the Seven Benedictions are recited and the couple drink wine, twice from the same vessel; then the bridegroom dashes the glass to the ground. Drinking the wine reminds the couple that they are required to share each other's pleasures and halve each other's troubles. The broken glass symbolises the weakness of marriage without love.

Before the ceremony is concluded, the following covenant is signed:

> 'On the ... day of the week, the ... day of the month of ... in the year ... corresponding to the ... of ... the holy covenant of marriage was entered into, in ..., between the bridegroom, ..., and his bride, ...
>
> 'The said bridegroom made the following declaration to his bride: "Be thou my wife according to the Law of Moses and of Israel. I faithfully promise that I will be a true husband unto thee. I will honour and cherish thee; I will work for thee; I will protect and support thee; and will provide all that is necessary for thy due sustenance, even as it beseemeth a Jewish husband to do. I also take upon myself all such further obligations for thy maintenance during thy lifetime as are prescribed by our religious statutes".

'And the said bride plighted her troth unto him, in affection and with sincerity, and has thus taken upon herself the fulfilment of all the duties incumbent upon a Jewish wife.

'This covenant of marriage was duly executed and witnessed this day according to the usage of Israel'.

QUAKER WEDDINGS

When a Society of Friends wedding is to take place, the arrangements come under the care of the Society's registering officer for the area concerned.

It should be noted that besides giving notice to the registering officer, notice must also be given to the local Superintendent Registrar in the usual way.

The Society's registering officer will ensure that the Quaker regulations are followed and that, if they are satisfactorily completed, the meeting for worship to solemnise the marriage is duly approved.

At the ceremony, the usual custom is for the bride and bridegroom to sit surrounded by their relations and friends, and then for the two to stand at a moment when they feel it is right. Holding hands, the man makes the following declaration:

> 'Friends, I take this my friend, ..., to be my wife, promising through divine assistance, to be unto her a loving and faithful husband so long as we both on earth shall live.'

The bride makes a similar declaration. A certificate is then signed by the couple and two witnesses, stating that the couple made the necessary declarations, that they fulfilled the legal obligations and were duly married. All those present are invited to sign the certificate after the meeting is over.

No ring need appear at the ceremony, but sometimes one ring is given or rings may be exchanged after the declaration.

WEDDINGS ABROAD

A fairly recent innovation is to travel abroad to get wed. There are travel companies who will arrange the whole package deal for you. The favourite destinations are some of the islands of the West Indies, the Seychelles, Mauritius and Mexico. It could be seen as travelling to your honeymoon destination first, then getting married.

Some couples may take members of their family or friends with them, but if they arrive alone the travel companies may organise a best man and bridesmaids, in addition to all the legal arrangements, hotel and travel, and 'extras' such as flowers, wedding cake, reception and video of the ceremony.

If the idea of marrying abroad appeals to you, but you would prefer to make the arrangements yourself, you should be especially careful. The problems you might encounter are numerous and will involve you in a great deal of correspondence with the various authorities.

6

THE RECEPTION

After the wedding ceremony comes the reception and in the case of the traditional English wedding this follows a certain pattern. It may be a very large reception with hundreds of guests or a small, informal gathering, but in either case there is a very similar pattern to the proceedings.

The first decision regarding the reception, which needs to be made some months in advance of the wedding, is where the reception should be held: hall, hotel or house. With a large number of guests, the choice is between hall and hotel, and in either case an early booking will be necessary. An average size house can probably accommodate only 30 or 40 guests, but there is an attractive alternative if the house has a large garden. It is possible to hire marquees which can be set up a few days beforehand and which contain all the necessary fittings such as lights and wooden or mat flooring.

A decision about the catering arrangements will probably be made at the same time as the choice of venue is decided. Naturally a reception held in a hotel will mean that the hotel will arrange everything at an inclusive charge per guest. It will also provide rooms in which the bride and groom will be able to change their clothes during the reception.

Unless some members of the family are particularly adept at catering, it is probably wise to call in specialist caterers, whether the reception is in a hall or a private house. It might seem feasible to lay on a tasty spread for 30 or so guests in a small, informal gathering at home, but with a hundred and one other things to think of on the big day, the professional touch can often be worth the extra cost. A booking in a local hall no doubt provides the most options: outside caterers or do-it-yourself, sit-down meal or buffet. What the hall might not have is a suitable room in which the bride and groom can change into their going-away outfits, so a suitable arrangement will need to be made.

A Formal Reception

A formal or semi-formal reception will have a receiving line to welcome the guests. This usually consists of the bride's mother and father, the bridegroom's mother and father and the bride and bridegroom themselves – in that order. This applies whether or not either set of parents is divorced. New partners are not normally included in the receiving line. The best man is not always included as he is usually the last to leave church, but if he does arrive in time he should be included after the groom.

Each guest is greeted by name or by politely asking their name. The bride and groom introduce each other to the guests when necessary or convenient. Generally it is sufficient for each guest to identify themselves to the first in the line. This is the traditional way, but today receiving lines tend to be more spontaneous and faster moving. If a large number of guests has been invited and you want to speed up proceedings, the bride and bridegroom can do the receiving on their own.

On entering, the guests are usually presented with a glass of wine or an aperitif, and when the last guest has been received everyone looks at the seating plan to find out where they are placed. The toastmaster (or best man) guides the guests to their seats. The processional order is: bride and groom, bride's father with groom's mother, bride's mother with groom's father, chief bridesmaid (with best man if he is available), bridesmaids, page boys, ushers, then guests. Sometimes seating arrangements are left to the guests to make their own choices. If there are separate bar and dining areas, early arrivals can wait comfortably in the bar until everyone is assembled.

Seating arrangements vary according to the number of guests and the layout of the tables. For a formal reception, however, there will be a 'top table' for the principal members of the wedding party and the attendants (see Checklist 6.1). Since it is an honour to sit at the top table, be careful not to hurt anyone's feelings by including a guest who is not also a member of the wedding party. An aunt who has flown in from Australia for the wedding may, however, be classed as an exception!

The bride and the two mothers usually work out how best to seat the other guests. If there are complications due to a parental divorce, seating arrangements at the top table should be discussed with all the parties concerned. Depending on how co-operative they are likely to be, there should be no problem in finding everyone a place. You will probably want to aim at some interchanging between the families, but not so much that no one knows what to say to each other.

If traditional arrangements seem inappropriate the solution may be to have a room full of separate tables: this can create a much more relaxed and successful atmosphere as long as the guests are grouped tactfully with a good mix of men and women.

If the bride's parents are divorced and she has been brought up by her mother and a stepfather, he may be asked to make the first speech and propose the main toast. However, the exact arrangements will vary according to the individual circumstances and should be discussed and agreed beforehand.

The most important thing is that personal feelings about ex-partners do not get out of hand and interfere with the success of the wedding. If the situation is handled with dignity and understanding, there is no reason why they should.

If a minister is present they must be invited to say grace and should have been approached in advance. If there is no minister present, grace may be said by the bride's father, for which the best man or toastmaster requests silence. The bride and groom are the first to be served or to serve themselves.

After the last course is over (or alternatively, about halfway through proceedings), the cake-cutting ceremony and the toasts and speeches take place.

If there is no official toastmaster present, the best man introduces the speakers.

The first to speak is the bride's father who stands and says a few words before proposing the main toast: 'Health and happiness to the bride and bridegroom.' The bridegroom responds briefly, thanking the bride's parents and the guests, and ends by proposing a toast to the health of the bridesmaids. The best man follows by replying for the bridesmaids and reading out the congratulatory telemessages and cards. The bride may also elect to say a few words.

All the speeches should be kept short and informal. If they can be witty without being offensive, so much the better. However, a sincere approach often goes down just as well, so if you have any doubts about your abilities as a humorist, it is best to avoid jokes!

The cake should have been ordered some weeks before and delivered to the reception on the day of the wedding. Icing on a traditional wedding cake can be very thick so it will help if this is already cut through. The bride holds the knife in her right hand, with the bridegroom's right hand on hers, and her left hand on top. After the first slice has been successfully dealt with, the cake can be taken away and cut into smaller pieces for the guests to eat with their coffee. You may wish to rescue the top tier to keep for a christening. Use cake boxes to send pieces of the cake to people who could not attend the wedding.

If there is to be dancing, the bride and bridegroom will be first on to the floor, followed by the chief bridesmaid and the best man, then the parents of the bride and groom and members of the two families.

After a while spent chatting to the guests, the couple slip away to change into their going-away clothes, returning for a few minutes to say their final goodbyes before going on honeymoon. Traditionally, just before they leave, the bride tosses her bouquet to a bridesmaid or a young female guest who, tradition has it, will be the next in line for marriage.

At the end of the reception the best man collects the groom's clothes and checks that nothing has been left behind by male guests. He ensures that the wedding cards and any messages are returned to the bride's mother. The host, hostess and best man are the last to leave.

CHECKLIST: SEATING PLACES AT THE RECEPTION

Arrange seating plan ☐

Top table

1. Groom's mother
2. Bride's father
3. Bride
4. Bridegroom
5. Bride's mother
6. Groom's father
7. Chief bridesmaid
8. Best man
9. Groom's family
10. Bride's family

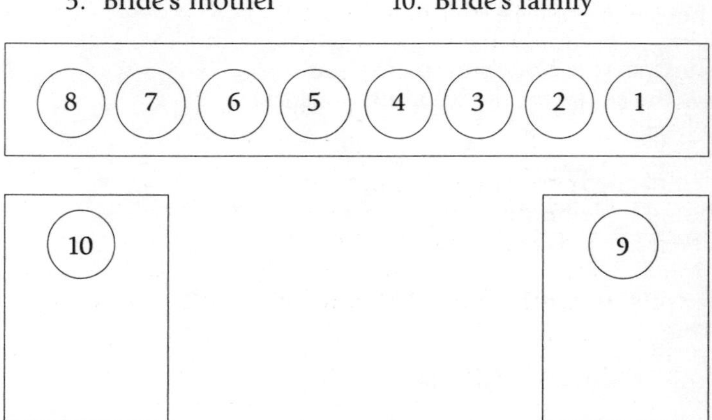

Variations on the seating may be made, although the top table is usually reserved for the wedding party. Alternating the sexes is usual. The families can be mixed.

CHECKLIST: AT THE RECEPTION

As the guests arrive they should be greeted by:

- The bride's mother and father ☐
- The groom's mother and father ☐
- The bride and groom ☐

Attendants and ushers should offer drinks and chat pleasantly ☐

The best man guides guests to the seating plan ☐

The hostess (the bride's mother) should give the signal for the wedding breakfast to begin ☐

If champagne is used for toasts only, it should be left until after the meal and served just before the speeches begin ☐

The best man or toastmaster requests silence for grace ☐

The minister or the bride's father says grace ☐

After the meal, the best man or the toastmaster calls upon the bride's father to speak ☐

The bride's father gives a speech and proposes the toast to 'The bride and groom' ☐

The bridegroom responds, gives a speech and proposes a toast to 'The bridesmaids' ☐

- [ ] The best man responds on behalf of the bridesmaids, gives a speech, reads out a selection of telemessages and cards and gives the programme for the rest of the reception
- [ ] The bride and groom cut the cake
- [ ] The bride and groom lead the dancing, followed by the chief bridesmaid and the best man, and the parents of the bride and groom
- [ ] The best man oversees the decoration of the going-away car, ensuring that no damage is done
- [ ] The best man organises transport for the bride and groom and hands over the documents
- [ ] The bride and groom change into their going-away outfits
- [ ] The best man places the luggage in the going-away car
- [ ] The bride and groom say their goodbyes
- [ ] The bride tosses her bouquet

7

THE HONEYMOON

If the wedding ceremony and reception need careful thought and planning, so does the first trip that the bride and bridegroom will take together as a married couple. Most people will want to have a honeymoon, and the tradition of beginning the honeymoon immediately after the wedding is still followed by many couples today.

Apart from the question of cost, the most important factor is to take a honeymoon which will appeal to both of you. A honeymoon in which the interests of one partner are followed while the other trails along with little enthusiasm is hardly the best way to start married life. So there should be a discussion well before the wedding; read through the brochures together, and book the holiday well in advance.

When thinking about where to go for the honeymoon, remember to take into account the date of the wedding. If you are getting married in the winter months, and you want sun, you will have to pay for it. Alternatively, you could opt for a honeymoon in a city, such as London or Paris, where the attractions are not so dependent on the weather.

Do not be shy about admitting your new status: some travel firms offer honeymoon trips complete with free champagne and four-poster beds, and hotels will often make a special effort to see that the honeymoon stay is as enjoyable as possible.

Honeymoons abroad also mean you have to check on passports, travel tickets, travellers' cheques, hotel reservations, foreign currency and medical insurance, as well as any inoculations that may be required. Do not leave it all to the last minute. You will have enough to do in the run-up to the wedding without worrying about the possible after-effects of an injection against cholera!

Finally, do not be too surprised if the honeymoon does not live up to all your expectations. The first few weeks of marriage are rarely without their problems. Two adults who have already developed personalities and ways of their own have to learn to adjust to one another. Relax, take things as they come, and you will soon find yourself looking back with affection on what will almost certainly be one of the most memorable holidays of your life.

8

WEDDING SUPERSTITIONS

Most of us like to play the superstition game at one time or another and weddings, in particular, come in for a whole range of sayings and warnings - which are fun if you take them with a pinch of salt!

When it comes to deciding on the date it is considered unlucky to marry on your birthday; however, it is considered particularly lucky if husband and wife share the same birthday, although they must be a year or two apart.

The Bride

There are many sayings related to the bride. The need for her to wear 'something old, something new, something borrowed and something blue' at the wedding is well known. It is generally considered unlucky for the bride to make her own dress - even professional dressmakers rarely do - and it is even more unlucky to try on the full bridal array too soon, especially if she sees herself in a full-length mirror. She can, of course, leave off a glove or a shoe out of respect for the old tradition!

Did you know that an old veil is thought to be luckier than a new one? This is particularly true if borrowed from a woman who is happily married, or if it is an heirloom from the bride's family. The good fortune and/or fertility of the earlier marriages pass with the veil to its new wearer.

The colour of the bride's dress is supposed to be a faithful portent of the future:

White is a symbol of purity and virtues.
Green typifies youth, hope and happiness.
Red is a sign of vigour, courage and great
passion. (There may be a touch of jealousy, however.)
Violet denotes dignity, pride and high ideals.

The wedding procession is not overlooked. The bride must leave her home by the front door with her right foot foremost. It is considered lucky if the sun shines, if she sees a rainbow on the way, or meets a black cat or a chimney sweep 'in his blacks'.

The modern custom of sending a piece of wedding cake to friends and relatives not present at the reception has its roots in a desire for them to share its luck-bringing properties. One old saying advises the bride to keep a piece of the cake; if she does her husband will be faithful to her.

The following dates are reckoned to be especially lucky for weddings:

January	2	4	11	19	21	
February	1	3	10	19	21	
March	3	5	12	20	23	
April	2	4	12	20	22	
May	2	4	12	20	23	
June	1	3	11	19	21	
July	1	3	12	19	21	31
August	2	11	18	20	31	
September	1	9	16	18	28	
October	15	18	27	29		
November	5	11	13	22	25	
December	1	8	10	19	23	29

Other superstitions about the wedding day are of a more general nature.

- 'Happy the bride whom the sun shines on' may be a well-known saying. But did you know that one thing said to guard against rain is to feed your cat on the morning of the wedding? (If you're getting married in Germany, however, steer clear of cats. Each drop of rain is looked upon as a blessing on the marriage.)

- It is a good sign if the bride is woken on the day by the song of a bird, and also if she discovers a spider in the folds of her dress!

- It is bad luck to break anything – especially a mirror – on the wedding morning, or to lose the heel of a shoe.

- With each glance in the mirror, the bride is supposed to add something to her make-up or clothing, even if it is only a pair of gloves.

- It is bad luck for the couple to meet in the morning before the wedding, but good luck if they smile at each other when they meet in the church.

- A bride is not supposed to weep before the marriage, but she may do so as much as she likes afterwards; this proves that she is not a witch, who could shed only three tears from her left eye.

- If the bride sees a lamb, a dove, a spider, a toad, or a black cat on her way to the church it is a sign of good luck; but it is reckoned a very bad sign if she encounters a funeral party, or if a pig crosses the road in front of the wedding car.

The Bridegroom

Rather fewer superstitions surround the conduct of the bridegroom on his wedding day.

All will be well as long as he does not see his bride in her wedding dress before he meets her in the church, and does not drop the ring before putting it on her finger. If she has to help him in this, he may expect to be ruled by her in the future. It is also considered unlucky to buy the engagement and wedding rings on the same day.

The bridegroom should pay the church fees (through the best man) with an odd sum of money, carry a small mascot in his pocket and on no account turn back for anything after leaving for the church.

After the honeymoon, the husband should carry his wife over the threshold of their new home. When this is done, both will be rewarded with all the good fortune they could wish for.

The Bridesmaids

Finally, for the bridesmaids, there is one very well known saying: 'Three times a bridesmaid, never a bride'.

9

WEDDING ANNIVERSARIES

Most people like to celebrate wedding anniversaries with presents and perhaps have an evening out at a favourite restaurant or theatre.

Traditionally, certain materials are associated with individual years in the course of a marriage, the idea being that anniversary presents in those years should be made out of those particular materials. So, if you want to uphold the custom – flowers and boxes of chocolates notwithstanding – the list below gives the materials generally associated with each year. They do vary slightly, however; paper is sometimes given for the first year, leather for the twelfth, ivory for the fourteenth, wool for the fortieth, and silk for the forty-fifth.

Anniversary	*Wedding*
First	Cotton or Paper
Second	Paper
Third	Leather
Fourth	Silk or Flowers
Fifth	Wood
Sixth	Sugar
Seventh	Wool or Copper
Eighth	Bronze
Ninth	Pottery
Tenth	Tin

Anniversary	*Wedding*
Eleventh	Steel
Twelfth	Silk and Fine Linen or Leather
Thirteenth	Lace
Fourteenth	Ivory
Fifteenth	Crystal
Twentieth	China
Twenty-fifth	Silver
Thirtieth	Pearl
Thirty-fifth	Coral
Fortieth	Ruby
Forty-fifth	Sapphire
Fiftieth	Gold
Fifty-fifth	Emerald
Sixtieth	Diamond
Seventieth	Platinum
Seventy-fifth	Diamond

Notes

ADDRESSES

Supplier

Address

Telephone Fax

Supplier

Address

Telephone Fax

Supplier

Address

Telephone Fax

Supplier

Address

Telephone Fax

Supplier

Address

Telephone Fax

Supplier

Address

Telephone Fax

Supplier

Address

Telephone Fax

Supplier

Address

Telephone Fax

Supplier

Address

Telephone Fax

Supplier

Address

Telephone Fax

Supplier

Address

Telephone Fax

Supplier

Address

Telephone Fax

Supplier

Address

Telephone Fax

Supplier

Address

Telephone Fax

INDEX